Namaste *the* HARD WAY

namaste
the HARD WAY

A Daughter's Journey to Find Her Mother on the Yoga Mat

SASHA BROWN-WORSHAM

Health Communications, Inc.
Deerfield Beach, Florida

www.hcibooks.com

Library of Congress Cataloging-in-Publication Data
is available through the Library of Congress

© 2018 Sasha Brown-Worsham

ISBN-13: 978-07573-2060-6 (Paperback)
ISBN-10: 07573-2060-0 (Paperback)
ISBN-13: 978-07573-2061-3 (ePub)
ISBN-10: 07573-2061-9 (ePub)

Publisher: Health Communications, Inc.
    3201 S.W. 15th Street
    Deerfield Beach, FL 33442–8190

Cover and interior design and formatting by Lawna Patterson Oldfield

TO MY ONLY REAL GURU AND TEACHER:
MY MOM. SUSAN SCHAEFER BROWN.
YOU ARE MY FOREVER MYSTERY.
MAY MY CHILDREN FIND
YOUR WISDOM, SPIRIT AND STRENGTH
ON THEIR OWN MATS SOME DAY.
IN EVERY BREATH.
IN EVERY POSE.

Contents

Introduction

This is my story of yoga, death, pain and discomfort, growth and presence, and being reborn even in grief.

A yoga class consists of various steps. We arrive and start to center, often on our backs. We let outside concerns float away and notice the little pains and discomforts we have brought with us. Then we start to notice the breath, the rise and fall of hands on our chest and belly, the gentle pull and push that keeps us alive but that we rarely focus on in the way it deserves.

This breath is life.

Next we move, connecting that breath to the body. We undulate the spine in cat and cow postures, or we twist, lying supine on our backs. Each inhalation provides a chance to strengthen and embolden. Each exhalation is an opportunity to surrender and melt a little deeper.

Eventually we find the top of the mat—Urdhva Hastasana (upward salute). We reach for the sky, then dive down to the earth. After sun salutations, we begin to flow from one pose into another.

As much as vinyasa practice is linear, it is also fluid. A strengthening posture may lead to balancing, surrendering, or opening the heart. It mirrors life. As children we live in the moment, as yogis we live fully present. We have little time to reflect, and so we rarely do. As we grow and have more time behind us, we begin to see all sides: our past, present, and future. In a practice, as in life, we flow from one to another. We try to remain here now, but we drift and move. Our past informs our future. So it is in this book. The lessons and spiritual path of my life continue to overlap. The more we examine pain, hold it, and breathe through it, the more we grow. Maybe it's Utkatasana (chair pose) or a death in the family, but grief and discomfort offer their own lessons. They have so much to teach us if only we open ourselves to them.

1. centering

THIS IS THE MOMENT WE HIT OUR MATS,
WHEN THE LIGHTS DIM AND STUDENTS
BEGIN IN SILENCE, OBSERVING THE BODIES
THEY HAVE BROUGHT WITH THEM,
AND HOW THEY ARRIVED.

Fastest Girl in the 'Hood

For the first ten years of my life I am the fastest girl in the neighborhood. We live just outside downtown Dayton, Ohio. The houses are roughly twenty feet apart, three-bedroom homes with one-and-a-half bathrooms and small yards. For my parents, as with most in the neighborhood, our home was a starter, the kind newly-weds bought in Ohio in the late 1970s for $19,000, wondering if they could afford it.

Then the kids start coming, first in a house two doors down, then next door. I am born next, on July 19, 1977. More children follow, one after the other, year after year, except in my house, where my parents wait almost nine years to have my sister. The neighborhood kids are like siblings to me. We play all day in the hot sun, pile like puppies into our parents' cars and drive to the pool, where we spend hours dunking each other, swimming to the bottom, and doing handstands with eyes so wide open they stay bloodshot all summer. At home we play hide-and-seek outdoors well past dark, catching fireflies and tackling each other until our parents scream for us from their front porches, long after the streetlights have come on.

It is a magic that later generations of kids may never experience, in a world of seat belts, child abduction stories, and dirt phobias, with parents so attentive that one can hear the whirring blades of their concern, like a helicopter circling over a traffic jam.

In the midst of all this, my mother discovers yoga.

On the afternoons I spend at one house or another, she is meditating. She had dabbled in meditation and some version of yoga back in her New York City days, before I was born. A close friend of my parents introduced her to George Gurdjieff, which led to meditation circles and eventually to yoga.

But this was long before I was born, even before my parents packed up their Brooklyn Heights rental apartment and moved back to their shared home state, Ohio, so my father could attend law school at the University of Dayton. They bought the small house on the corner of Burbank Drive and Audrey Place for $19,000. At the time it was a financial stretch, but they loved the details of the two-story brick house: the built-in formica kitchen table that jutted out from a built-in display cabinet, the cute sunroom off the dining room, the large room over the garage where my father could place his father's former law school desk, the walls he lined with books and papers, and the small sewing room, which served as a catch-all space because no one in my family could sew as much as a button onto a shirt.

These decisions were made long before me. They spent three years in this house while my father gutted out his classes and eventually passed the bar. There is a photo of him in his black cap and gown at his law school graduation. He has long hair and a long beard. He looks a little like a short, stubby Rasputin. Beside him, my mother is dressed all in white, and her belly is so big she looks as though she might topple forward. It's the only photo I have of her when she was pregnant with me.

They put me in the sewing room for the first few months of my life—or so I am told. By the time I develop any conscious memory, I am in the large bedroom right beside theirs, with blue walls, a blue carpet, and a closet big enough to store all kinds of things, including my pinafore dresses, Christmas decorations, and my father's vast pornography collection, which was initially stacked safely in a box marked "Ashley's things" in the top right corner of the closet. It takes me many years to find all those *Playboy* magazines, stuff them into a duffel bag, and distribute them on the school playground.

My parents buy me a water bed, which becomes the talk of the neighborhood. Kids come in and out of the house to jump on it and ride the waves. Another kid's house has a basketball court, and another's has a swing set. One kid has a garage full of old screws and pieces of wood that we use to build forts.

The three children next door—Sarah, Josh, and Beth—are my best friends. Adam and Amanda Burden live in the next house down. Next to them is David, whose parents hang Confederate flags all over the house and eventually move after a black family moves in across the street. There is also Little David, Betsy, Caroline, her younger sister Maura, and many others.

Around this time my mother starts attending a meditation group, and those children are added to my circle as well. While the parents prop their hips on pillows, ask for silence, and breathe, we run in the backyard, organize races in the middle of the street, and tie wagons to the back of bicycles so we can carry our friends from one house to another.

When I run I tighten the fingers of each hand into a blade that slices through the air, making me even speedier. I beat all the boys in our daily road races and dominate in the ghosts in the graveyard game and in hide-and-seek, too. I imagine myself winning Olympic medals, and I am sure I am the fastest girl in recorded history. My entire body is made of skin, bones, and muscle. I am tiny and compact (before my breasts make their dramatic appearance), and I am so willowy that my mother is often asked if she is feeding me enough.

I love banana nut pancakes and the sugar cereals my father sometimes sneaks into the house. I love pudding pops, chocolate cake, tuna noodle casserole, and chicken with peaches on top. I love broccoli, salad with Italian dressing, and pizza with black olives. I love breakfast at my Catholic Nana and Bampa's (my maternal grandparents') house best because they let me have bacon and they make their French toast carefully, not the way my mother does.

She is lazy when it comes to cooking, and her French toast always has cooked egg whites around the edges. Even though I love French toast, I don't enjoy being reminded of what's inside. It seems as if a disgusting secret is being revealed. It should taste eggy and buttery *without* revealing its secret. This is, perhaps, the only time I throw fits about food: when my mother makes breakfast with burnt toast, rubbery eggs, pancakes that are runny inside, and French toast with fried egg bits hanging off the plate—all specialties of the house. Somehow I still grow. I become stronger and faster and taller, although the latter takes a while, burnt toast and all.

Running is my thing. I feel freest when my arms are pumping and my heart is thudding in my chest. I love this sport at which I can beat the boys. I like running until I feel like vomiting. I love the feeling of the wind, the dripping of the sweat, the pounding of my feet. I love running so fast that the wind whistles in my ears, and I especially love blasting music on speakers and running up and down my block over and over.

I join the track team later and become a sprinter. Only through trial and error do I learn to really love long races of endurance. I find out that I am better at pacing myself over a long haul and that my fast-twitch muscles, the ones I use to power over hurdles and beat the boys in the 100 yard dash are actually much weaker than my slow-twitch muscles, which power me over distances.

I love to make my heart pound and my breath go faster. I love to move, shake, dance, and climb.

I have trouble sleeping because I am scared of the dark and because my heart and my mind are always racing. At night, when my mother puts me to bed, she teaches me to meditate. At first we try it quietly, the way she likes it.

"Focus on your breath," she says. "Imagine that your breath is a beam of light you pull in through the nose."

I do, but it's hard. What happens to this light? Does it stay, or does it leave on the exhalation? My breath is faster than my mother's. I pull my breath in, and it stays, but then I need to exhale before she gives the command. I am red-faced, trying to hold my breath, focusing on that space between one breath and the next and bursting with the stress of that.

"Imagine your exhalation as black smoke, releasing all the bad stuff."

"There's bad stuff?"

I imagine monsters, killers, blood, and all the things my mother won't let me watch on TV or in the movies.

"Bad stuff like anger," she says, "or things that keep you awake. Now *shh*."

I quiet myself down, imagining the ocean and sinking into the warm waves. But then I think of Jaws. My mother has just gone on a yoga retreat, and my father has taken me to see one of the sequels. I imagine that shark living in my water bed. I am sure that I have the one water bed in history that somehow connects to the ocean and has a shark.

"Mommy, are there sharks in water beds?"

"No. *Shh*. Focus on the breath."

But I keep imagining that shark. In landlocked Ohio, sharks aren't a legitimate concern. I should fear tornadoes and Confederate flags in this part of the state, but that doesn't stop a six-year-old mind from racing.

"But what if mine has them?"

"It doesn't."

"But what if, Mommy? What if?"

"Then we'll get you a new bed."

I am satisfied for the moment. But just barely. Before I can focus on my breath, I am also thinking about cheese, about how my mom buys only white cheese you can cut from a block. My friends have orange cheese, the kind you peel cellophane from, the kind that melts easily on white bread, something else we don't have in my house.

"Why can't we buy the orange cheese?"

My mother sighs, and I know she's angry.

"Just go to bed," she tells me, lifting herself off the chair next to my bed.

"But the cheese, Mommy. It's so much better."

She finally snaps. Even yogis who meditate have their limits. And apparently orange cheese is hers.

"No. No, it's not. It's gross and processed, and it's not something I am going to buy."

"But all my friends have it. They have Kool-Aid and Pop-Tarts and Cinnamon Toast Crunch, and all I have is granola and water."

This isn't the first time we've had this discussion. Our pantry is a source of massive confusion for me. My friends have creamy salad dressings and not just vinegar. They have packets of colored sugar they can put in water to make it taste better. They have giant tubs of ice cream instead of small quarts. They have milk chocolate, not just dark chocolate. They have iceberg lettuce instead of the darker, leafier lettuces we buy. This is what I am considering instead of my breath.

"Just go to sleep," my mother finally hisses.

But I can't. My mind is racing. Sharks. Serial killers. Cheese. It's all in there. All connected. How does anyone breathe when there is so darn much to be stressed about?

Mom Can't Braid

"I want them to call me Sara."

I tell this to my mother, who is behind me, her long fingers groping through my thick mane of hair. She will stay there for ten minutes, braiding—just long enough to declare it done and for me to look in the mirror and scream at the result.

"How are you the only mom who doesn't know how to braid?"

She'll forgive me this rudeness because that's what moms do—and honestly, because the woman can't braid. Strands of hair are poking out from all over this two-strand monstrosity she calls a braid. A black hair tie with two plastic orange balls is wrapped around the end, and my hair is all twisted around it.

It's my first day at a new school in a new town, and it's a new way of life. Until now I've been in private school, a Montessori school where there was no homework and we called our teachers by their first names. Math was taught with beads, not worksheets, and the principal's name was Ginny. Until now, my school had been a small brick building where I spent all day painting, reading, and playing

12

with blocks. There were no grades, only long conferences between my parents and teachers at which words like *rebellious* and phrases like "possible emotional issues" were tossed around liberally.

In the third grade—that is, when I was eight years old (Montessori doesn't have grades per se)—I was sent to a therapist for orchestrating a walkout with my fellow students over some issue with the pizza we were served on Fridays. The teachers admired my moxie at Gloria Dei Montessori, or so they said. But I am sure they secretly applauded when the girl who once walked out the back door to view a crime scene two blocks away, which she'd read about in the paper, finally left for good.

In my new school, Northmoor Elementary in Englewood, Ohio, I would be switching classes. The building was slate gray, and I would have homework. Finally! Homework! I would have proper grades and plenty of structure.

I imagine rows of proper girls with braids in this suburban school, and I want to fit in. It was bad enough when my mom couldn't braid at Montessori, but at least we weren't alone. I was sure the moms at Northmoor would know basket braids and fish tails and all manner of elaborate side braids (it turned out I was right), so walking in with this two-stranded twist that looked like a cross between a bad soft-serve ice cream cone and a funnel cloud was not going to work for me.

"I hate you," I tell her, pulling the braid apart.

Three weeks from now we will go to her beauty salon and get my hair chopped off and permed with feathered bangs (Why, God, why?), but for now I will go to school with a thick mess of half curls and a scowl of discontent. I sure as heck won't be going with the name Sasha.

"Why do you want to go by Sara?" my mother asks.

I put a hand on my hip and roll my eyes with all the disdain a skinny ten-year-old with a concave chest and protruding ribs can muster.

"Sara is normal. I wish you had just called me that in the first place."

My mother smiles.

"Okay, well, we named you that because we liked it."

"Well, then, why did you call me Sasha?"

"Because we liked that, too."

Fair point. Until now, it wasn't something I questioned. I was Sara at the doctor's office and with my maternal grandparents, and I was Sasha everywhere else.

I won't be able to shake the name. On this first day of fifth grade, I am about to meet my future husband, although I won't know for more than a decade that that's what he is. And when we do meet again in Boston, where he has arrived for graduate school and I have been living for almost seven years with my father, he will tell me that everyone thinks I changed my name for show. "Like to pretend to be some kind of exotic, sexy person instead of just plain Sara."

He won't know that this decision was made here, in my small brick house in Dayton, Ohio, and that it was the braid that made the decision for me because I couldn't walk into a school ten miles away, in a smaller suburb, surrounded by tract housing with aluminum siding and girls named Tiffany, Jennifer, and Heather, with a shitty braid and a weird, foreign name. So I was Sara with no *h*, and even though I would take the name Sasha back a million times, I could never really take it back without being a poseur, and the worst thing one could be is a poseur.

Speaking of posing, my mother can stand on her head, but she can't form a proper braid. I wonder why there isn't some test mothers are given before they are handed their baby girls ("Must know how to braid and change diapers").

It makes sense. Later I will practice French braiding until my fingers are numb, and I will do it every day on Barbie dolls, friends, and eventually my baby sister, just so my two daughters will not suffer this extreme humiliation.

My mother is certainly amused with her little girl in her Coca-Cola shirt with acid-washed jeans and a Swatch around her minuscule wrist, insisting there is one way to be.

But there *is* only one way to be, and my mother isn't it.

Little Sara Brown marches into school on the first day. My homeroom teacher, Mrs. Truesdale, will tell us in health class when we are learning about our periods that her hysterectomy was the best thing that ever happened to her. My mother will frown and complain to the school. Mrs. Shearer will tell us during our unit on the Holocaust that Hitler wasn't all bad. I meet Krissy, the cheerleader; Mike, a little boy with perfectly slicked hair who is obsessed with cars; Shawn, the kind of wild boy who gets a D in everything and kisses Krissy at recess; and Heather, the blondest and most alpha female to ever grace the fifth grade.

Heather has a perfect French braid, so within a day or so we are best friends. Her father is a cop, her mother is a teacher, and they have miniature lop bunnies in their backyard, which sprawls over three acres and has a creek, only Heather calls it a "crick," and we catch salamanders there. "Your mom is really cool," she tells me later in the year, after she has opened up to us both about her parents' divorce.

My mother suddenly seems old, with her salt-and-pepper hair, and the baggy linen pants she picks up off the floor next to the hamper day after day seem gross. Then there are the strange sandalwood beads around her neck; the crystals in her ears, the ones with special powers to refract the light and charge her with creativity; and the leather-strapped sandals that highlight her pale toes and unpolished toenails. All of this comes to seem weird and witchy compared to the pretty young moms who populate our school community.

My friend Janet's mother isn't even thirty yet, and she's still in college. She hangs out with people who are barely older than we are and drives a cute two-door sports car. At my old school, the moms were like mine. They had marched in the 1960s and had the Birkenstocks to prove it. They were lawyers, activists, and city people.

My mom's lack of braid prowess is only one of her many failings. All of this happens because I change my name, because I am Sara ending with an *a* and without an *h*. I sometimes wonder what if I'd kept my name, if I'd been Sasha. It probably would be the same. After all, it's just a name. But somehow I imagine I'd be fiercer and less willing to throw my mom under the bus for the bright lure of popularity. The fact that she doesn't shave her legs or armpits every day, skips makeup, and never gets manicures will become part of a larger sense of shame about where I am from. I am embarrassed to invite people to my house and hear my parents call me Sasha. So I insist that they call me Sara, too. Although they are happy to accommodate my other requests in life, that's one I never get. Sasha I was and Sasha I will stay.

"Someday," they tell me, "you will be grateful."

They were right.

And my mother will never learn to braid. But I will.

Strange Breath

The strange breath my mother does is alternative nostril breathing, but I don't know the name yet. It sounds as if she is trying to blow her nose, and the thought of the snot swishing down from the nasal cavity makes me gag. My gagging is involuntary, but she rolls her eyes.

"Please be serious," my mother commands.

Her hands are in a V-shape, ring finger and thumb compressing her nostrils, while the sound whooshing out of her nose is more forceful than anything my eleven-year-old mind can conjure up when it comes to the word *yoga*.

"This is weird, Mom."

And it is. I am all long legs and energy. I am about trips to the mall and phrases like "gag me with a spoon." This yoga stuff is all too weird for me. To sit, even for five minutes, is too much to ask. And this embarrassing snot-filled breath is the cherry on this humiliation sundae.

"Why not just inhale and exhale like a normal person?"

She smiles and maintains her cross-legged position. It will be years before I know that this is called the lotus position, with her feet pulled in toward her groin in an X across her lap. It will be years before I realize how hard this pose is, one I am not built to master, and how it will be my nemesis.

Someone who was looking in the window would see a woman who is patient, loving, and understanding—or at least she is trying to be in this moment, trying to channel her guru and all the books she has read on raising children with love and patience. The observer would also see an ungrateful eleven-year-old tilting her head, mouth agape, eyes set to roll.

Of course this would be wrong. My mother is feisty, funny, and passionate, and when she gets angry the chill lasts for days. She's no guru. There is a current of electrified anger in her, and I know how to set it alight. She's volatile, and she can be violent as well. But right now she is determined.

She has learned this mindfulness breathing exercise at the ashram. She wants to share it with me, and she keeps trying, even when I keep failing.

"*Om mane padme om*," she chants.

"What the heck, Mom? What does that even mean? It sounds like gibberish."

"It means we want to be like Buddha," she says. "It means we sit in silence and hope for enlightenment."

"What's that?"

"Wisdom. *Samadhi. Shh.*"

My mind is all over the place. I don't know what *samadhi* is, but I am pretty sure I am one more question away from a smack on my arm. She's trying, but I know her buttons. I open one eye and look at her. That breath is so loud. It's ragged. It's chunky. It sounds like beef soup being slopped into a bowl.

Like Buddha? Not so much.

My religion goes more like this: On Sundays I'm dragged to Hebrew school while all my friends are in Bible school. I'm told daily that I am going to hell from friends who join the Royal Ambassadors of Christ instead of the Boy Scouts. Being Jewish is bad enough, but Buddha? Snot breath? Chanting in ancient languages? Definitely a ticket straight to hell.

"We don't believe in hell," my mom reminds me.

"Okay, so not hell. But something. This is weird."

"Try it."

She's encouraging me, holding out her hands. She takes one of my hands in hers and folds it the right way so I can bring it to my nose and breathe air in one nostril, then out the other.

"Why would I ever want to do this?"

"It's about balance. You need balance. You are focusing on your breath, so you are not focusing on other things."

"What other things would I focus on?"

"School. Homework. Friends' travails. All your usual stuff. Now shh."

My mother's study is quiet. It's our practice space, but it's also the only room in the house with a computer. I spend a lot of time in this room, and most of it isn't spent on yoga or meditation, either. The blue walls are calming, and there are built-in bookshelves along the whole front wall. The titles and authors mean nothing to me now, but someday they will mean everything.

Autobiography of a Yogi. Doris Lessing. Margaret Atwood. *The Yoga Sutras of Patanjali.* It will all come later. Now it's just mom's weird taste and a lifetime of embarrassment for me.

"You'd be so pretty if . . . " I tell this to my mother all the time. If she wore her clothes right side out. If she didn't pick the first crumpled pair of pants up off the floor. If she used a curling iron. If she dyed her hair instead of letting it go gray. If she wore her contact lenses instead of her glasses. If she shaved her legs. If she wore makeup.

Other moms read Tom Clancy and Danielle Steele. Other moms dye their hair red and drive little convertibles. Other moms breathe through both nostrils at the same time.

Other moms are normal.

My mother practices yoga early every morning. In the winter it is still dark, but right now it is spring and the light is starting to come in through the blinds on the windows. It is still too cold outside to open the windows, so the room is full of smoke from her incense burner in the corner.

It will be years before I go through my own incense phase, which will coincide with my tie-dye "wish I was Jamaican" phase. Now the smoke just burns my nostrils as I try to suck in some air. Her eyes are closed. She is focused. I am not. I fidget. I look around. I see the black-and-white photos of her guru. I grimace and start a mental makeover of him. *First I'd cut that long hair. It looks greasy, and his ends are all split and curly.*

There's not much to be done about his smile, which even at my age seems smarmy and sexual, as if he were hiding his true nature under a facade of peace and celibacy. He looks like a strange mix of hippie and priest, something I am sure appeals to my mother as a refugee of the Catholic Church who became a hippie but is still clearly seeking spiritual guidance, a set of rules that can govern her behavior and help her make decisions.

I only know that this guru makes my muscles tense, and I definitely can't focus on my third eye with that creepy guy looking at me. My mom is silent, her eyelids fluttering.

"Is there really a third eye?" I blurt out, breaking the silence. She doesn't answer. I wonder if my mother's knees hurt. I wonder how she keeps that posture. My shoulders want to slide forward, to curl toward the floor. I want to lie down. I don't understand silence. I want to dance and shout and sing and ask questions.

"*Shh.*" She places a finger over her lips. I hear the clock ticking.

Teaching Friends to Meditate

"**I** am going to meditate with your mom," Janet tells me.

She has just arrived. It's Friday night and she's staying over. I watch as she unpacks her bag, laying out all her clothing on the second bed in my room. We are waiting for pizza, and one of our favorite games is to dress up in our sexiest outfits and answer the door when it arrives. Janet has three pairs of cutoffs, each one shorter than the other; a T-shirt she cut the bottom off so it shows her belly button; and three Reduce, Reuse, Recycle T-shirts that are three sizes too small. Janet is at least a D cup, so when the doorbell rings I just hide in the staircase, giggling, while she does all the flirting and prancing.

This meditation thing with her is news to me.

Lately it's been hard to get her to come over. We just started high school, and Janet is in the color guard, the pretty girls who come out at half time with the marching band and twirl giant flags in rainbow colors while the band plays.

Our marching band is nationally ranked, which means that Janet is gone every weekend for games and band camps. She's also gone every summer for a couple of weeks for band camp, and she has a whole new crew of friends.

Janet is my best friend. We bonded in fifth grade watching *Dirty Dancing* every day after school. We shared a locker all through middle school and decorated it with wrapping paper and inspirational quotes. Her mother, Terry, is a decade younger than my mother and drives a sports car. Terry was only nineteen when she had Janet and finished college just as we finished elementary school. Terry has red hair and wears a bikini at the pool, and everyone agrees that she looks as good as any of the high school girls. She's also religious. Until fourth grade Janet went to Catholic school.

I was no stranger to church. I had been there with my maternal grandparents, who are Catholic, a few times, but I don't talk much about religion with the kids in my school, and especially not with Janet. I worry she will think we are sacrificing chickens and eating babies.

"Why would you want to meditate?" I ask.

"She told me it will help with boys."

"Boys?"

Yes. Lately another big divide between us has been boys. The summer before, her first one at camp, she started seeing someone. They kissed, and he felt her up under her shirt. Boys still make me uneasy. Although I definitely need a bra, I only just started my period a couple of weeks before high school. All those feelings my friends describe—the beating hearts, the flirtation, the giggling, and the excitement of it all—haven't happened for me yet. I am feeling left behind, and now Janet is talking to my mom and not me.

"Why are you talking to my mom about that?"

"Your mom is cool," Janet says, her gum cracking.

Her red hair is in a constant state of disarray, but it's part of her charm. She always looks as though she's just taken a ride on a static-filled plastic slide at the playground. But her laugh is infectious and loud, and she's always in a good mood and up for anything. She's in her underpants and bra, and there are rolls of skin around the sides of her bra. Everything about Janet is big: her personality, her hair, her body, her laugh. She's vivacious and fun, and my mother adores her. But still.

"My mom is not cool," I tell her. My mom teaching my friends to meditate is horrifying and embarrassing to me.

Janet holds open a pair of jean shorts and slides one leg in after the other. As she pulls them up, it's immediately obvious they won't button, but she is unfazed.

"On to the other pair!"

She pulls them from the pile on the bed.

"Your mom is just chill. She always knows the right things to say and doesn't stress when you tell her what's going on. She's way better than most moms. She's like the mom I would tell I was pregnant before I would even tell my own mom."

"Why would you be pregnant?"

"Ugh. Sara, come on. I am not pregnant. I am just using it like a 'for instance.' Like, for instance, if I were a teenager and pregnant, I would tell your mom because it like seems like she can handle that stuff."

I nod.

She manages to squeeze herself into the jean shorts, but the button is definitely threatening to pop. When she slides on the homemade T-shirt, she looks as ripe and juicy as an August peach. I am sure the pizza boy will love it. But I am still confused.

"Are you interested in meditating?"

"Kinda," she says, shrugging her shoulders.

Kinda? Okay.

"Me too," I tell her, even though up until now this hasn't been true.

The pizza boy turns out to be a man of at least thirty-five who stares at the corner of the living room the whole time he is at the door. Janet bounces and squeals anyway, trying to get his attention, but he is either uninterested or really clear about the fact that showing interest would make him a middle-age pervert.

We eat the entire large pizza ourselves while my sister dances and twirls through the living room in a Jasmine costume, singing songs from the movie *Aladdin*. *I can show you the world . . .*

The pizza guy doesn't know what he's missing.

"So do you girls want to do some yoga and chanting with me?"

My mom is wearing two strands of mala beads, made of sandalwood. At the bottom of one is a crystal. It used to hang in our breakfast nook and cast rainbows all over the kitchen, but now she wears it around her neck.

"No," I say at the same time that Janet says yes. I let Janet win, but I know she will see it. My mom is weird. I can see hair poking out from her too-short pants, and I cringe, remembering the conversation we had last week about shaving her legs.

"You don't have to shave above the knee," she assured me. "The women in our family don't grow hair there."

But I do. And she does. It looks as though she's decided to stop shaving altogether. As for me, I shave my entire leg. Each one. Every day.

We follow my mom into her study, where she has already rolled out three mats. She's burning incense and playing some strange chants. We sit, cross-legged, facing her.

"The goal is to clear the mind," she explains.

"Ugh, Mom, I know. I get it."

She tilts her head and looks at both of us.

"But does Janet know?"

She has a point. I quiet down.

"Focus on the space above your upper lip and just notice the way the air enters and exits there. Now, imagine a light, coming from the inside, lighting that exact spot. Keep focusing on the light and imagining the breath passing there."

I open one eye and look at Janet. She is quiet and breathing. Her palms are on her knees. Her eyes are closed. She doesn't look uncomfortable or embarrassed or as if she is about to tell everyone in school what a weirdo heathen my mother is. My mother is also breathing calmly. She has one hand on her belly and one on her heart. Her eyes are closed. Both she and Janet look so peaceful.

After we meditate, Janet has a lot of questions for my mother. How often should she do this? What are the benefits? How does yoga fit in with meditation? My mother answers them all, and then Janet asks about her malas.

"So are they like rosary beads?"

My mother nods. "They are exactly like rosary beads, only you use them for your mantra or your prayer. There are 108 beads, and you run your fingers over each one, saying your mantra until you get to the last bead, which feels a little different to touch."

She takes Janet's hand and puts it on her necklace.

"See how that one has a different shape? That's so you don't have to open your eyes when you get to the end. You can just keep on meditating."

"So cool!" Janet says, but she is getting bored. I can tell by the way she's shifting her eyes. I want to go watch a movie. The room feels smoky, and the incense is burning the inside of my nostrils.

"Thanks, Mrs. Brown," Janet says.

"It's Susan," she reminds her for the hundredth time.

Janet laughs, throwing her head back and showing all her teeth, her red curls bobbing.

"I'll never remember."

"Do you girls want to come with me next week to see Gurudev?"

"No," I say quickly. "Definitely not."

Janet is nodding vigorously. She points at the photo on my mother's altar.

"Is that him? The one with the long hair?"

"It is. He's from my ashram. He's amazing."

"I'm in," Janet says.

I am annoyed she didn't consult me. Annoyed that I have to feel annoyed with this. I don't want to go see Gurudev, and I feel so embarrassed that my mom is pushing all this on my friends.

"Don't you have a band thing?" I ask.

But she doesn't. It's an off week. So we are on. Great.

The next morning, right after Janet leaves, I barge into my mother's bedroom.

"Why would you ask Janet to do that next week?"

My mother is half dressed and is putting her prosthesis into her bra. The scar across her chest is jagged, and even though she doesn't snap at me, I am reminded. We are lucky. I should be grateful. But I am too angry.

"You are so embarrassing," I continue. "You know what her mom thinks of all this stuff."

"Honestly, Sasha, she seemed interested. If you don't want to bring her, uninvite her. It's no big deal."

"Are you going?" I ask.

"Of course I am," she replies.

The truth is, I am hurt that she invited me only because Janet wanted to go. I want to go. I don't want to go. I hate her. I love her.

The room is hot, and I am sweating. The sunlight pours down from the skylight over the bed, making a tunnel of heat right next to where I am standing. My mother finishes putting on her bra and pulls a shirt over her head.

"Also, you need to start knocking," she says.

"Since when do we knock in this family?"

I am right. She knows this. It will be years before I learn that in normal families, knocking is a thing. It's expected.

"Since now. You're fourteen. You're in high school. You can knock on the goddamn door."

She's right.

"Okay," I say. "And we will come next weekend."

"Good. I think you will like it."

"I doubt it," I tell her, and walk out the door, slamming it behind me.

What's in a Name?

I am at the Social Security office. I am twenty-five and married. The line is long and full of old men with long hair and beards. It will be years before *Duck Dynasty* becomes popular, but in 2003 these men are ahead of the trend. T-shirts hang off muscle-sinewed frames. The man to my left, standing a bit closer than I'd like, smells of aftershave and bacon, and his belly pokes out from beneath a plain white tank top. His jeans hang low, and he grunts every time we move up in line. The whole process feels like two steps forward and one step back.

I am here to change my name.

After months of deliberation, one huge party where I wore a strapless white dress, and a two-week honeymoon in the Dominican Republic, I have dealt with my identity crisis and have made a decision. My last name will be hyphenated. I know. Hyphenating a name is such a cop-out. Brown is the name I've had my entire life.

The pros of keeping it: I am always near first in any alphabetical list. It is the first name under which my byline has ever appeared. I met my husband in the fifth grade and used to mock his last name:

Worsham. In the hills of Appalachia, to "worsh" is to get a bundle of dirty clothing wet and soapy, preferably (though not definitely) in a "worshing machine." Brown is simple. It tells you nothing about me. No ethnic background. No details that would make you think of me any differently. My name is Sara Brown. It doesn't get more generic and simple than that. Google is not yet a thing, but later, no one will be able to Google "S Brown" without a million hits, drowning any embarrassing personal information under a mountain of cooking advice from one Sara Brown or hair-braiding tips from another. Brown is a pretty sweet mask. You have nothing on me. It's anonymity in a name.

The cons of keeping it: I love my new husband. I want us to be a family. I want the same last name as any children we have. This is true even though I cringe every time I hear the full last name I will take. Even now.

The pro list is longer, so I choose to split the difference, which is why I am standing in this line that feels more like a game of chutes and ladders than an efficiently run government office. Someone is weeping in the corner, and the crowd blocks me from seeing her face, but I silently connect. I have no idea why she is crying, but I feel her pain. Four hours in a South Boston Social Security line could break anyone down.

When my name is finally called, I have my birth certificate, my Social Security card, and everything else I think I need.

And then the inevitable: A woman with ink-stained fingers and glasses that slide down her nose pushes my stack of identifiers back through the glass window separating us.

"Your gas bill here says 'Sasha,' but your birth certificate says 'Sara.' Which is your name?"

"How much time do you have?" I ask her.

She stares back. Apparently jokes are a no-go at three o'clock on a Wednesday afternoon.

But seriously, lady. The story is complicated.

"Are you looking to change both your names?"

I look back at the line behind me and wonder. Maybe this is the time to end a lifetime of this question: Are you Sara, or are you Sasha?

My birth certificate says Sara Mariasha Brown. I've checked it several times. But from the day of my birth, my name has been Sasha.

My mother chose Sara because it was biblical, and when she was confirmed into the church at age fifteen, she'd chosen Sara as her confirmation name. The other choice, the story goes, was Rebecca. But my parents, in their hippie wisdom, never called me Sara a day in my life. Minutes after I entered the world I was Sasha.

"It sounds like a DP," my grandmother told my mother. A displaced person was one of the many Jews, Gypsies, and other refugees who had been left homeless after World War II. My mother and her mother refused to call me Sasha. To them I was Sara.

Who knew that these two names—the one my parents never could have anticipated on the day of my birth, when I was just a soft-haired bundle in a flannel blanket—could cause so much unintentional confusion?

Years later, when I named my own children, I came back to this. Two out of three of them have nicknames. Samara is Sam, and Adara is Dar. But having a nickname is different from being two distinct people. It's different from this push and pull of two cultures, my father's Russian Jewish one and my mother's Italian American, Catholic, middle-class one.

The woman at the Social Security office is waiting for my answer.

Do I want to change my name? Do I want to finally let Sasha take the wheel? One thing I know for damn sure is that I never want to have to come to this office again. The choice feels like now or never. I have thought about it a lot. It makes sense. It's time to finally embrace being Sasha Brown-Worsham. Legally.

No more having to say "Sara is my legal name, but Sasha is my nickname" to every person who sees my credit card. No more feeling like a liar when I say my name is Sasha. No more store clerks asking to see my driver's license to verify that I am, in fact, the cardholder purchasing these five tomatoes and a pack of vitamin drinks.

"I don't respond to Sara," I tell people, but I also know that this is not entirely true. I respond to Sara in certain situations, like at the doctor's office or when I am checking out of a hotel. Sometimes at the gym where I teach yoga, my name comes up in the system among people who don't know me.

In fact, they are two different women. Sasha's hair is wild and untamed. It falls past her shoulders in wide strips of disorganized curls. She loves sex and only wants to talk in depth. Friends tell her their stories: the time their mother lied to them, their brother's cocaine issues, their grandmother's anger. Sasha is the kind of person who loves astrology, charges her crystals, and reads tarot under the full moon. When Sasha teaches yoga, she asks her students to moo and meow and "move your body in any way that feels good." She encourages people to close their eyes and feel the rhythm of the beats. Sasha is sexy. Sasha listens to Sade and Jim Croce and doesn't find anything weird about those competing genres sharing tracks on the same playlist.

Sara's hair is straight from her weekly blow-drying. She loves shopping. She's definitely judging you. Sara talks like a Valley girl and says things like "gag me with a spoon," "like, OMG," and "Can you believe she wore that?"

Both Sara and Sasha are genuine. To change my name legally to Sasha would be to choose one side of myself over the other.

I don't tell the woman at the Social Security office any of this. A woman with only one name would never understand.

And so I say: "No. I'm Sara. And Sasha."

Five names, five realities.

First Crow

"**I**f you get one toe off the ground, you are a baby crow."

I am long past the dislike I had for my mother's yoga. Baron Baptiste, the yoga instructor, is talking to me from the television in my father and stepmother's lake house in Maine. I stay here every summer for almost a month. It's my favorite place on Earth, with a rolling stone terrace, an acre of wooded land, and an expansive lake with a dock and boats and several kayaks. My children and I feel at home here. But, unlike at our home in New Jersey, yoga is hard to find. There are no studios close by. I take my practice inside. But I only have the one Baptiste video, so I do it again, and again, and again—the same poses every day.

I am stuck in Bakasana, a permanent baby crow, with one toe perpetually off the ground. One afternoon in 2014 it all comes together. My toes touch behind me. I engage my *bandhas* (inner strength). I pull up on the muscles for urination and those in my low belly, and I lift off.

I am flying. I am hooked.

Later I will wish I had a better story for how I became a teacher.

The truth is, I wanted to do it as soon as I walked into the Baptiste studio in 2004. I looked at the prices every month. I considered the training. But it was always too expensive, and I never felt good enough, so I always put it off. *When I have my handstand. When we have the extra money.*

The Baptiste training was strange; it seemed like the road to actually teaching in the studio was paved with four $5,000 fees and four different levels of training. None of that was realistic.

Then I had my first baby. For a while my practice went in and out of my life, but now it has become daily. My last baby is now eight months old. My other two children are seven and six years old. There is space.

I read obsessively about yoga. "Practicing six days a week can change your life," one book promises.

And so I do. Each day I wake before the kids do. I roll out my yoga mat and move. But it isn't until I succeed in doing the crow posture that I finally start to see the benefits. Here it is, what I've been waiting for. Five years and hundreds of attempts at this pose, and finally one day it arrives.

As a teacher, I am used to the frustrations of my students. "I just don't feel like I am getting any better," they often say.

This is when I tell the story. People expect to practice every day and see small improvements, but with yoga sometimes the improvements happen all at once—like practicing the crow almost every day with no progress and then suddenly leaping right into it without issue on a sunny Wednesday in August.

Rob, my husband, mocks my pants. I bought them three weeks ago, and they look like someone's Grateful Dead–inspired acid trip.

"Did you buy those at the David Lee Roth collection?" my husband asks.

I roll my eyes. My yoga pants collection is growing. By the time I start a daily practice, I have forty-five pairs. By the time I become a teacher, I will double that. It's possible I am a hoarder. But I love all the different styles that suit my changing moods. There are neons and paisleys. I have six pairs of black leggings. Three are plain, and one has lacing down the sides. The last pair has laser-cut flower designs that flow and dance all the way down the sides of my legs.

My mother had two pairs, and they were loose and wide. Mine are all fitted.

"Your ass looks good," my husband tells me as I leave for a class at six o'clock in the morning. This is not my mother's yoga. But it is my addiction, especially after the crow.

I take more classes at the gym, but when that isn't enough, I join the local studio. Baker Street. It is small and intimate. Only twenty people can fit inside at a time, and each teacher has a unique style of interpreting the practice. Unlike any of the studios where I have practiced before, this one does not have a branded form of yoga. It's just vinyasa and up to every teacher to play with as he or she likes. Sonia's class on Tuesday plays with spirituality and a lot of dharma. Claire's is a gradual buildup to a peak pose that kicks your ass, but you don't know it because the burn is so slow, like frogs being slowly boiled to death without any pain. Heather's 5:45 AM class is the most challenging. I never leave without feeling as though I've showered in my clothing. Every pose is ten breaths long. My muscles quake and shake and scream, but Heather's adjustments are sublime. She presses on my lower back in a revolved triangle—a pose that is at once a lengthening of the torso and a twisting of the spine.

"Feel the crown of your head lengthen away from your tailbone. Now press into your left hand," she says. I feel the sense of length that allows for a stronger twist. I can see my top hand. I wiggle my fingers. Hello.

Of course, there are things I don't like, too. Teachers forget to take us through both sides of the body. They leave poses out of a sequence. Sometimes in the middle of class, Heather screams, "Sasha, honey, extend, extend. Length on both sides of the body. You are collapsing."

I don't enjoy being singled out, but it makes me a better student. And it makes me want more.

"We are spending a lot on yoga," Rob tells me. He's right. I buy multiple mats, one for home use and one for going back and forth to the studio, as well as one that packs up well for travel. My monthly pass at the studio is $150, and we spend $300 a month on our family gym membership. "It's excessive," Rob says.

I try to picture quitting the studio and focusing just on the gym, but it's not enough. The yoga there is fast-paced, set to music, and includes a long free flow, in which students just move to the music. Baker is entirely a guided practice. I love both styles of yoga, but the slow, guided practice at Baker would be hard to give up.

"Maybe I should train to teach."

It's the first time I say it out loud and with intention. Up until now I have only imagined it, thought it, played at it. But saying it to Rob as something real feels different. I explain that the $4,000 investment in the teacher training will quickly be earned back, and it gives me a second career option. Best of all, I will practice for free anywhere I teach, at the gym we love and at Baker Street.

This is how I sell it to my husband. But I know the real story: writing the same old things is getting old. I have worked for a women's website for more than seven years. The jobs have been good to me, and I have enjoyed them and loved the people I have worked with, but I am older now, and writing about young babies and sex and marriage is getting boring. My life has taken a new turn. Most days I'd rather be in the yoga studio doing back-to-back classes than writing yet another reaction to the day's news.

Yoga is water to the Internet fire. Writing on a website as a woman is complicated. Every essay I write is met with hostile comments.

"You should die in a fire."

"You never should have become a mother."

"You are just a JAP and no one likes you."

"I feel sorry for your husband."

These attacks roll off me, but at a cost. They change me. I hate people. I get angry. I snap at my family and look warily at strangers.

In yoga, we sometimes do the following *meta* (lovingkindness) meditation: *May I be safe. May I be happy. May I be strong. May I be at ease.* We send these wishes to ourselves and then to someone we love. We offer them to a stranger and finally to someone we dislike. Thanks to my work on the Internet, the latter two categories have fused.

Spending my day being attacked by strangers is hardening my heart. Yoga is softening it again.

Rob agrees that teacher training is a good investment. I start researching. There are a thousand different programs offered today. When my mother became a teacher, there were only one or two options. Now they are everywhere. I am overwhelmed by the possibilities. Jivamukti is my favorite style of yoga and they offer intensive options in exotic locations for $7,000. But you have to commit to veganism. There are some great local studios close to me starting teacher training in the spring. But I already feel old. I am thirty-seven, and I've already waited so many years. I want to be teaching by the spring, not just starting a yearlong program.

I search until I find a 300-hour program through Flor Yoga in Jersey City, just ten minutes away. We have lived in New Jersey for a little over a year, and it isn't home yet. I still get nervous driving to the mall, and I use a GPS to find the kids' extracurricular activities. But something tells me this is the right one.

I e-mail. Sarah, the head of Flor Yoga, gets back to me right away. "You sound like my mother," I tell her.

It's a done deal. Sarah owned a studio in Manhattan for years. She closed it after 9/11, but yoga is her heart and soul. We connect immediately. Her concept of yoga is one of connection, of slow practice with quiet music. Whether a person eats animal products or has a six-pack of beer is hardly the point.

"You want them to have a spiritual six-pack," I tell her.

She laughs. She gets me. I'm in.

The program starts with 100 hours of yoga for pregnant women. It's my first introduction to teaching. This section is mostly full of practicing teachers who are using this as continuing education. The program runs Wednesday and Friday nights and every other weekend for three months.

"When you leave, you will be able to teach mothers-to-be as well as the general population," Sarah tells me.

It feels like fate, as if Google put this exact course here. Now. For me. But of course I know this isn't the case.

That night I practice alone in the living room. Rob is in England and the kids are asleep. I light a candle and place my hands in Anjali Mudra (prayer), my thumb knuckles pressed into my third eye. I ask for Guidance. Wisdom. Strength.

I am nervous. I am ready. I am in the Tabletop pose, my hips over my knees and my shoulders over my wrists. I look down at my hands.

The veins are starting to pop. When did that happen? I want to believe it was when I was still in my twenties, when my hands were soft and young. In that case it's not a sign of aging. But I know it's recent, just in the last year or so.

I remember my mother's hands and the popping veins—even before she got sick. She must have been the same age I am now. I recall her stroking my cheek, holding my hand casually on my knee during a performance of *Annie* on Broadway.

"Will my hands have veins like this, too?" I ask, taking her hand in mine and stroking her palm with my index finger.

"Someday," she says. "No time soon."

Soon is now, I think, as I look at these hands. Soon is now.

I roll over my toes, press my heels toward the ground, and push my belly toward my thighs in the Downward Dog pose. Home base. Breathe in, breathe out.

2. Breathing

BEGINNING WITH A FEW
CLEANSING BREATHS, WE THEN EVEN THEM,
LEADING EVENTUALLY TO THE UJJAYI,
A VICTORIOUS BREATH THAT BECOMES THE
METRONOME FOR OUR PRACTICE.

How My Parents Met

"**A**re you talking to me?"

The pretty woman with the long brown hair and curvy body speaks to the man at the table next to her. She is a freshman in college in 1967 and a little heavier than she will be in five years. Her face still has a little bit of baby fat, but her high cheekbones and strong jaw are striking. "Good bone structure," people say. And they are right. She has thick hair and a wide smile with perfect teeth. Her laugh is infectious, and although the man (whose name is Ashley) wasn't talking to her, he wants to be.

They are at a campus coffee shop in the basement of the Christian Student Union at Bowling Green State University in Toledo, Ohio. Ashley, in an old brown suit and with thinning hair, is small in stature but full of charisma and charm. He's known as a rabble-rouser, someone who enjoys causing trouble and is loudly opposed to the war in Vietnam. He has written articles for the campus newspaper and stood on podiums with a bullhorn, screaming his opposition to all things conservative and stodgy.

43

He's someone the woman (whose name is Susan) wants to know. She will be my mom and he will be my dad.

We later joke at the differences we see between them in old photos: my father, Mortimer Nerd in his suit and tie, who claimed one should "always look professional when you protest so they don't think you are just some druggie," and my beautiful mother, radiant with long, thick hair. They made quite a pair.

Later that night they went back to a dorm room with the two friends they were with, Nick and Diane. They listened to Phil Ochs and maybe they kissed. The next day Ashley called and they went on a date, even though it was a month before summer break and my father was set to spend it in Brazil with a former girlfriend, learning Portuguese and traveling.

They wrote letters every day, and when my mother received one in July she claimed that her father told her, "You got a letter from that Jewish boy." Even though my maternal grandparents were wonderful and I adored them, that story burned its way into my memory. That Jewish boy. It's not the last strange thing someone in my mother's family will say about our Jewish side.

My mother came from Parma, Ohio, a part of Cleveland known for being 93 percent white, the kind of place where the reputation of being so white can precede everything else.

"I am from Parma," my mother would say, and the listener would nod sympathetically.

"Oh," everyone would say.

She'd nod.

I learned what this meant in the back of my maternal grandmother's brown Oldsmobile.

We are at the mall, sitting in the parking lot while Nana pulls out her sunglasses. An old friend of hers is in the front seat next to her. I don't know him. A man passes on our right, wearing a fur vest, his hair spiked and gelled.

"He's a little queer," Nana's friend tells me.

"Queer?"

"Soft. Gay. Queer."

My uncle, my father's brother, is gay. Until now I've been told that boys can marry boys sometimes and girls can marry girls sometimes and that it's no different from any other couple. This makes sense, but *queer* as a bad thing does not.

Later, on the drive from Cleveland to Dayton, I tell my father about this conversation.

"And how did that make you feel?" he asks.

"Sad. Sad for Uncle Mark."

Mark is Dad's younger brother by ten years and by far one of my coolest relatives. He has been with the same man since college. Mark and Bobby live in New York City in a tiny walk-up on the Upper West Side. At this time the neighborhood is sleezy and full of hypodermic needles and misery. When I spend the night at their apartment, they let me stay up late and cuddle their cats, and they play Clue with me for hours.

My mother was the oldest of four children. Her closest sibling in age is my Aunt Mary, who is Mom's polar opposite: a perky blond cheerleader with a million boyfriends. The next youngest, my mother's brother, Joe, is a star quarterback who will undoubtedly go to a Division One school for college. My mother and her youngest sister, Patti, have the most in common, although with ten years between them it will take a while for this to become evident. Both will move to New York City and become yogis. But growing up in Parma, no one was a yogi. Not yet. They were Catholic.

My mother received all the standard sacraments. A photo of her first communion is in my study now, yellowed and precious, her white dress perfect, her shoes shiny, and her hair a thick helmet of hairspray and holding gel—just as Nana would have ensured. They went to church every Sunday and tended to be Democrats. My grandfather was a union man. With only his salary as a lineman at the illuminating company, all four kids nevertheless went to high school and then eventually college and graduate school. My grandparents played bridge and went to church and dressed all four of their children perfectly for every holiday, with matching dresses for the girls on Easter and fluffy red coats at Christmastime.

They cared about what the neighbors thought.

My grandmother was the daughter of Italian immigrants. My grandfather's family was German, but they had been here longer, and he didn't like to talk about them. Nana was a force, funny and brash and bold, with a thousand opinions. She gave the best hugs and always made me feel incredibly special, mostly through food.

There were pizzelles at Christmas, carefully cut-out sugar cookies with perfect frosting. We had handmade pasta and meatballs with a "secret ingredient" (raisins) that sweetened the sauce just enough. Bampa was a cook, too. He made fluffy pancakes and "soldier eggs" that he cracked into a hole in the center of a piece of bread. He loved a glass of scotch after work, served in a stained-glass cocktail tumbler with at least one maraschino cherry.

He used to peel apples for me perfectly when I came to visit and put a small bowl of potato chips out for the cousins, with dip, which was carefully spooned from the bowl. They cared about those small details, which make you feel immensely loved.

When my mom was ten her parents built their dream house with a garage door opener, a front porch, and an expansive backyard leading right into a creek. Every house on the block was the same prefab style, with two and a half bathrooms. It was a short walk to the high school and slightly longer to the mall.

When my mother came home that summer after meeting my father, no one was thrilled. It made sense. My father's family was the opposite, geographically and in every other way. My paternal grandparents lived in Cincinnati, at the southern tip of the state, across the river from Kentucky. My grandfather, with his slicked back gray hair, made a name for himself by defending Jim Morrison and Larry Flynt against obscenity charges. He defended Ku Klux Klan members and their right to burn crosses on city property, and once he took me to jail to meet a client he was defending on a murder charge.

He was voted the "worst-dressed man in Cincinnati," by *Cincinnati* magazine and wore pastel polyester suits and patterned shirts. He also had a mistress for more than twenty years, which was an open secret among all three of his children.

Unlike my maternal grandparents, my paternal grandparents didn't care what the neighbors thought.

Despite their different family backgrounds, my parents fell in love.

We Caught It Early

While my mother is dying, no one is being honest about it. "They caught it early," my mother tells anyone who asks how she's doing, and my sister and I believe her.

During the first half of summer, I get my first job as a counselor at the day camp I went to as a child. I am also getting my driver's license. I turn sixteen in July and spend all of May and June in driver's ed so that on my birthday I can go to the Department of Motor Vehicles and get my temporary license. In Ohio, a temporary license means I am allowed to drive anywhere I want as long as I have a licensed driver with me. Of course, the licensed drivers I choose are my friends who have had licenses for five days, two months, six months, with one senior friend.

In other words, I spend the entire summer flirting with death.

As a camp counselor my main job is to keep the four-year-olds in my care alive, awake, and entertained from the moment their parents drop them off at the big brown lodge in the back of the Jewish Community Center to the moment they pick them up. We do arts and crafts. We play flag football. We lower the flag. We sing songs. We raise the flag. We sing more songs. We dance.

For two hours every day the kids take swimming lessons. I sit by the side of the pool, providing an extra set of eyes while the lifeguards teach them the breaststroke, the doggy paddle, and freestyle, and the kids dunk their little heads without fear.

I am never seen in a swimsuit, though. I wear baggy sweatshirts and long shorts because finally, after praying and hoping and wishing and begging, I get my wish. My breasts have arrived—and how: 34DD.

Be careful what you wish for. I refuse to be that girl. There are so many "that girls" at the pool that summer. One is visiting from out of town, and all the male counselors have their eyes on her. She's stacked, too, at least a 34DD, with a tiny waist and long blond hair. She also has a giant nose and cheekbones, which I tell my friend make her look like she was formed from Legos, but no one is looking at her face.

She immediately starts dating the boy I had my eye on, so of course I hate her. Meanwhile, the hottest lifeguard is a boy I knew in elementary school. Back then he was a dork, a tall skinny boy who hit me once with a crossing-guard stick. I told on him, and we became mortal enemies. One day my mother came to class to host a Halloween party. She told me he was a special boy and that maybe some day I might like him. I was sure she was wrong.

But now here he is: tan, built, and with a chest so broad and strong that it's easy to imagine him tossing giant logs long distances. But he's not a lumberjack. He's a lifeguard. I tell my girlfriends I hate him even as they drool. I don't realize that in ten years, almost to the day, I will marry this lifeguard in a ceremony in Boston.

"I mean honestly, could he be more obvious? 'Look at me, I am so hot.' Blah, blah, blah." This is my mood that summer, which is why I am especially frustrated when the director of the camp pulls me aside. She's heard about my mom.

"We just want to tell you how sorry we are, and if there is anything we can do, we want to do it."

"Sorry about what?" I am genuinely dumbfounded. What have they heard?

Carol, the director, tilts her head a bit and looks quickly at Amanda, the assistant director. Did she say something wrong? I can tell this is what she is wondering, as if I should know what they are so sorry about.

"Well, we heard." She's fumbling with her fingers, looking at the ground behind me.

"She's sick. Correct? She has cancer? No one told us until now. We just wanted to let you know that we see how you talk about her. We see how much you love and value her. We hope that our daughters think of us that way, too."

Amanda is nodding, and they are making eye contact now. They both lean in. They want me to know how sincere they are, but I honestly can't understand why I am in the office having this conversation.

The cancer? Really? "They caught it early. She'll be fine," I tell them.

I am repeating that line like a mantra. But at home I wonder if it's true. My mother is weaker than I have ever seen her. She's tired all the time. She takes long naps. My grandparents are staying longer and longer in our house to take care of her. The doctors are saying the medicine isn't working as quickly as they'd like.

Still, my mother keeps saying this to me. "We caught it early."

I don't know. I don't know that a recurrence of cancer is practically a death sentence. I don't know that at this point we are looking at months and not years of life left. I don't know any of this because I keep being told that "we caught it early." It's not true. She has stage IV metastatic breast cancer, and the pain she feels in her bones is the cancer depositing itself there and multiplying every day. But I don't know this, and I resent this conversation with the camp directors.

"She's fine," I assure them. I believe it's true, but the conversation nags at me.

Later, I am watching Rob, that hot lifeguard. Who does he think he is, anyway? I am grateful for the distraction, though, if only for the moment, because what Amanda and Carol said keeps weighing on me. Is my mother sicker than she says she is?

There are signs. Most nights she is too tired to make dinner. We eat bagels or call for a pizza. I am not especially magnanimous about these adjustments.

"Get up and stop being so lazy," I tell my mother as she curls into the couch. She has another headache, and she tried to go swimming earlier in the day but had to come home because of pain in her bones. My father is due home that night, and my grandparents left two days ago. My mother isn't taking care of us, and I am angry. I am fifteen.

"Mariel needs you," I insist, knowing that I am hitting where it hurts.

We order Chinese food, and I slam the dishes around while setting the table. There will be dumplings, beef and broccoli, and moo shu, and I want to be sure the table is all set since my mother isn't getting up to help. When my father comes in, my sister and I run to him. She is full of hugs and love. "Daddy! Daddy!"

But I am angry. "Finally," I tell him, as he hangs up his coat in the closet. "Mom is on the couch."

By the time he gets to the living room my mother is crying. "I need help," she cries, her face contorted in anger, her cheeks wet. She's yelling. But I am more disturbed to see her cry. The last time I saw her cry was when her mother was diagnosed with breast cancer. That was four years ago, just before her own first diagnosis. After Nana told her, my mother placed the phone in the cradle and sobbed. Later I went into her room, where she was hunched over the bed, on her knees, her shoulders shaking with sobs.

"Mom. Mom. Mom." I repeated this because I didn't know what else to say. She looked at me, and I wanted to hug her. Her eyes were red and swollen, and I had no idea what she was feeling, but I wanted to curl up and tell her that Nana would be okay. But she shook her head and screamed. "Get out!"

I know what she thinks: crying is weakness. Seeing her like this reminds me that I am a complete shit. "I'm sorry." It's all I can think of to say. I know I have a lot to be sorry for. I am sorry for not taking out the garbage when she asked me the day before. I am sorry for not playing with Mariel the previous afternoon when my mother needed a nap and I insisted on going up to my room instead.

I am sorry. I am sorry. I am sorry.

My father is sorry, too. At least I think he is—he doesn't actually say it. But he does clean up the dishes after dinner, which for him is a big step and maybe shows how sorry he is that he's been in India for three of the past four weeks while my mother has grown sicker and sicker and sicker.

That night she and I go into her study and start to practice yoga, which by now I have become interested in. Even though I still love to run and jump and get my heart rate maxed out, I also love to move through the Sun Salutation and hang my head in Downward Dog. But tonight we start in a seated position. We meditate. And while we are pressing our thumb knuckles into our third eyes, we are chanting, "*Om mane padme om.*"

I am also praying in English. *Please let this be a blip. Please let my mother get better. Please don't let this end like this. And please let her know how sorry I am for being a selfish jerk.*

After we move and practice with a lot of breaks for the Child pose, she is sitting straight-backed against the wall, her legs folded in the lotus position. I sprawl across the floor and put my head in her lap.

"Are you going to be okay, Mom?" I need to know. I want the truth.

"Of course I am, honey. They caught it early."

I know she is lying, but I want to believe her. I want more than anything to believe her. "I love you."

"I love you, too." She pauses and thinks. "Can you leave before the second session of camp?"

I laugh. Of course I can. It's a silly summer job. Carol and Amanda will be annoyed, but they will understand. At least I think they will. "Sure, I guess. Why?"

"I want to take you and Mariel to Kripalu. I want to do this special program."

She seems to want to say more. I wonder, then quickly push the thought aside, if what she wants to say is that this may be the last time, the last chance—her last trip to Kripalu, and she wants to make sure Mariel and I go with her so we will have it in our memory.

"Yes," I tell her. "Let's go."

And so we do.

Samskaras

After you taste an apple for the first time, you know what it will taste like when you see an apple again. You can imagine that taste and know what to expect.

According to ancient Indian philosophy, *samskaras* are the thought patterns and scars that arise from our personal pain. A *samskara* is formed in the unconscious mind. It can generate a memory of the apple as well as an understanding of its taste, smell, and texture. The knowledge and the object become the same.

And so it is with our pain. The cuts happen in real time. We feel them. They make us bleed. But it's the scar tissue we build around them, the thick part we can't feel, that hurts us the most because when we can't feel the pain, we don't know when we've gone too far. We don't know when we've hurt people. Hurt people hurt people because we carry those scars with us.

Samskara 1

The worst night is not the night my mother dies, but the night my aunt tells me she's going to. I'm sixteen. My father has been traveling, and my Aunt Patti is staying with us. Sometime early in the morning, my mother spikes a fever, and by noon she's burning up. By six o'clock in the evening, my father has rushed home and admitted her to the hospital.

"Watch your sister," my aunt tells me, calling from a pay phone in the lobby. My father is with her in the intensive care unit. "She's probably going to die."

"What?" I say, thinking I had heard wrong.

"She's probably going to die tonight."

I still think I must have heard her wrong. The bagel with tuna salad I've just eaten is turning in my stomach. I am nauseous. My knees give out. I fall to the floor.

"What? What? What?"

My aunt hangs up, and I am alone with my sister Mariel. Mom doesn't die that night, or the next one. Five days later she comes home in a wheelchair with a big smile.

"I'm okay. I am going to get better. Don't worry."

Samskara 2

"If I die, I want you to keep living in the moment. Not feeling sad all the time."

My mother tells me this from the hospital bed we've moved into her study. She can no longer climb stairs, and this is easier than having someone carry her upstairs every night.

The cancer, which started in her breast, has spread to her bones and to her brain, and she is blind in one eye. As we talk, she squints in my direction. I am not sure if she can see me.

I am telling her about Chelsea, the "new girl." She just moved to town from New Jersey with her father, sister, and stepmother. A few days ago I told her about my mother, and she told me she lost her mother to ovarian cancer.

"They caught my mom's cancer early," I told her, and even as I said it, I knew it sounded crazy. Her cancer had metastasized (spread), which is the definition of stage IV, although I didn't know that then. She's bald. She weighs eighty-nine pounds. She sits in a wheelchair. She sleeps in a hospital bed. She's blind in one eye. But that's our story, and we are sticking to it.

Even though I believe my mother will live, I need Chelsea.

"It's awful," she whispers. "I have cried myself to sleep every night for three years."

She hugs me, and I think that this can't be me. This won't be me. I can't cry every day and every night for three years. I tell my mom this story while I sit in her study. She's in and out of sleep and on heavy pain medication, but tonight she's lucid enough to talk, and I need her to tell me the truth.

"Are you going to die?"

"No, I am not. But if I did, I wouldn't want you to cry every night. I would want you to get over it."

I try to imagine what it means to "get over it." None of us have any context for this. My mother is forty-five, and her mother is in the kitchen pureeing butternut squash in the blender so my mother will have food to reject later that night. Losing a mother isn't in anyone's plans.

"I need to know," I say. "This is bad."

"They caught it early," my mother says.

I believe her. I hate her. I know she's lying. I want her to live. I want to believe. Maybe that's why I don't believe what I see with my own eyes. Cancer in the bones doesn't disappear. Cancer in the brain doesn't get better.

My grandmother comes in, holding the tray with the food and a small vase with a geranium. Nana is full-service.

"I want things to be pretty," she says.

She cleans the house. She vacuums the rugs. She cleans the cat litter. She puts fresh flowers in every vase and reads to my mother from her favorite Dick Francis novels. She and my grandfather are exhausted. My father is away, and my mother requires full-time care.

Samskara 3

I go out every night with friends and drink and try to pretend that none of this is happening. I kiss random boys. I start to smoke more pot. My grades slip, but all my teachers feel sorry for me, so no one says a thing.

"It's awesome," I tell my friend. "I never do a thing, and they still give me an A."

My house is overrun with my mother's sisters, her brother, and my grandparents. I love them all, but they are not there for me and my sister.

"Why do you have to go out every night?" my grandfather yells. "It is stressing your mother."

He is a large man, at least six foot two, and when he hugs me he mashes me against his body, hits my back, and calls me Rascal. He peels an apple in one perfect ring and gives me potato chips in a perfect porcelain bowl. He is love. But his face is flushed. His jaw is tight and stern. He calls me selfish and tells me I am killing her faster.

"I have to get away from you guys," I yell.

My heart hurt. My heart breaks. But it's true. I can't be in this house. Or this body. Or this brain.

"Where is your father?"

I know the question is rhetorical. We all know he is on a business trip. He is working, I answer anyway. "He's in Paris. Someone has to make money."

I'll be damned if I'll let my grandfather be angrier than I am.

My father comes home. My grandparents leave. My mother has two weeks to live.

Samskara 4

"If you do die, I want you to visit me," I told my mother. "I want to know you are okay. I want you to watch me."

"Okay, I promise."

"I mean it. Send me a sign. Tell me you are okay. Don't leave."

She promises. It's the last time we talk about death. Soon after, my mom stops talking to me at all. On my fifth day at school, I get a card from her study. She's in the house, but she isn't. She calls me Sara. It's in my grandmother's handwriting.

"I hope you had a good first few days of school. I want to hear about it someday."

When I go to tell her, to sit with her, my grandmother tells me to leave and to take my seven-year-old sister with me. "It's too painful for her."

It's painful for us, too. I want to say this. But instead I say nothing and just stand outside the wooden door, my knuckles itching to knock but choosing not to. What is behind that door that I can't be part of? My mother moans in pain. I turn around.

Samskara 5

I have a big test in advanced placement biology. I've been studying for days, and Andrew, a boy who is acing this class, is in my basement, helping me study. He's tan, and his hair is long. He has perfect eyebrows, flawless teeth, and a certain swagger when he walks. His father is a neurosurgeon, and his mother is a glamorous socialite. They live in the nicest part of town, and he has two equally perfect siblings and a movie theater in his house. He is also the best student in AP biology. I am the worst.

I know he is here to support me, to be nice. But I can't understand why my mother is dying, why I don't have a movie theater at home, and why I suck at AP biology.

"I heard you had really bad acne last year," I say to Andrew.

"Yeah. So?" His lips are tight. They say tread lightly. They say I am on to something that might set him off. I nudge a little harder.

"I bet it looked pretty bad. I can't really imagine you with cystic, gross zits all over your face. Pretty lucky your dad can get you the best medicine."

"What? Because you are poor?"

"Not poor. Just not spoiled like you. If I had acne, my dad would make me tough it out."

"Sure. Whatever."

He backs down. I am the untouchably pathetic girl with a sick mom, and he knows better than to blow up at me. But I am not finished.

"Your senior quote this year is really trite," I state. "I mean, it suits you. But it's trite. 'Love many, trust few, learn to paddle your own canoe.' Really? I mean honestly, a kid as smart as you can't think of something that sucks less?" This time I've got him.

"Fuck off," he says.

He grabs his books and shoves them in his backpack. He walks out with his perfect hair and his stupid smile, and I am sure (and I am right) that in ten years he is going to be an investment banker in Manhattan, he will be rich and obnoxious, and I will hate him even more than I do right now.

I am going to fail the biology test. I don't care.

"You are on your own," he says, as he walks out the door.

Samskara 6

That night, my mom gets so sick that I don't have to go to school the next day. I hear her from my bed, moaning in pain like a cat howling, and everyone is so busy with everything that they probably don't hear her. But I do. I've heard it for days. It's not a cry. It's not a whimper. It's something else. I never want to hear it again.

The lights from the ambulance wake me up, and I hear voices downstairs. My father comes in my room.

"They are taking her to hospice. Do you want to come say good-bye?"

I am not tired. I am wide awake. But I turn over in my bed. No, I do not want to come. I pretend to be asleep. My dad is crying. I say nothing.

I am thinking it's the last night she will be in our house, and in my bones I know it's true. I know she is going to hospice, and even though I have been promised it's only for a little while, I know better. Hospice means death. I know enough to know that.

Within twelve hours she is dead. I miss her death by fifteen minutes. The next day, when I do go to hospice, I stop by our old house first. It's the place we lived for the first ten years of my life. The good place. I leave the car running, and I cry as I watch the new family inside. They have young children who run in and out. That tree—I climbed it a hundred times, and I remember my mom watching me on the tippy-top branch and telling me to be careful, to take it one step at a time, to breathe, to focus. I remember the round table and the red couch. I remember the yellow wicker furniture in the sunroom and the perpetually messy hall closet. I remember the banister where I kissed my father between each pair of uprights every night as I went to bed. I remember her bedtime stories and her fingers in my hair, working it into a soapy lather.

I remember. I remember. I remember. It becomes a prayer. I *remember*.

And then it *is* a prayer. My shoulders are shaking. I put my hands together. Anjali Mudra. I press my thumb knuckles into my third eye. *May they be safe. May they be happy. May they be healthy. May they be at ease with the conditions of their lives.* It's a prayer for the new family.

Because I send this prayer to them, I miss my mother's last breath. I miss my grandmother holding her hand. I miss the death rattle. I miss it all. My father greets me outside the front door. "She's gone," he tells me, holding my hand as he leads me to the room. I can't remember the last time he held my hand like this; I think I must have been a child.

I fall to my knees when we walk in the room.

"She looks just like the day she was born. Bald and perfect," Nana says, as she kisses my mother's forehead.

They leave me alone in the room, and this is all I can think: *May she be safe. May she be happy.*

Samskara 7

News travels fast, and Andrew calls me that night. He's awkward. He tells me about the biology test. I don't mention my mom. He knows. He finally gets to the reason he called.

"I'm so sorry about your mom," he says. "And I am sorry about our fight. I was a real dick."

He wasn't. I was the dick. Yet I reply, "Yeah. You were a dick. You are a dick. But it's okay. I'm fine."

I want to say I'm not fine, that they caught it early. I want to say it's all good. But I don't because I finally know they didn't. And I finally know it isn't.

3. connecting

WE MOVE THE SPINE AND
THE HIPS IN GENTLE WAYS, CONNECTING
BREATH TO BODY.
INHALATIONS HELP US
STRENGTHEN AND EMBOLDEN.
EXHALATIONS HELP US
SURRENDER AND ACCEPT.

Me as a Teen Versus Mom as a Teen

My mother kept hundreds of journals. After she died, the notebooks, legal pads, and stacks of paper with typed entries filled four giant moving boxes.

She started keeping a journal when she was fourteen. Later she found those notebooks in her parents' garage and cackled with glee at some of the entries. She spread the notebooks out in front of her like a picnic on my grandparents' plush pile carpet, reading some of the entries aloud. Some were funny. Some were not. A neighbor of hers had gone to fight in Vietnam, a newlywed with a baby on the way. They must have been close because she filled pages talking about him and his family.

Andy is leaving and everyone was crying at his going away party. I hope I am able to send candy to him over there. I am so worried. Several pages later, there was this: *My God. It's the worst news. Andy was killed in Vietnam. Everyone is so sad.*

Not every page was tragic. My mother was in a group called MIND. My mother can't remember what the acronym stands for.

"Something intellectual, something, something," she explains. I am laughing so hard I nearly pee because I'm thirteen years old and can completely imagine my dorky mother, with her long brown hair, Coke-bottle glasses, and a general disdain for sports of any kind. She and her friends were the kind of children I laugh at now.

I imagine my mom like Lori, who is in several of my classes. Her glasses go from far below her cheekbones to well above her brow line. Her brown hair is stringy and untouched by gel, mousse, hairspray, or highlights. She doesn't spray Sun-In on her damp hair and sprawl on her back deck, hoping to be just a little blonder. She walks in the halls, undaunted, with a book in front of her, leaving her prone to bumping into lockers and people, especially as the crowd swells between bells.

I like Lori. She is interesting. In our classes we talk about books we have both read and the lessons we are going over. But in the halls I never say hello to her. However, I don't call her names or tease her for being "nerdy," like some other kids do. Yet I am aware of the hierarchy and my tenuous position on the ladder. I would never jeopardize it by being seen with Lori.

I spend hours getting ready for school. I spray my bangs into submission and wear designer clothing. In Ohio in 1991, "designer" clothing comes from the Limited and Pasta—mock turtlenecks and tights under shorts. Southern Ohio will never have a fashion week, and most of what people wear is about ten years behind the magazines. But it's important to look the part of a popular, successful middle school girl.

My mom does not fit this narrative. Now, looking at her journals, it's clear that MIND was uncool in the extreme. But my mother isn't embarrassed at all. She's laughing in the way she sometimes does, her head thrown back and then forward, doubled over, with tears running down her face.

Her group wore capes to school and tried to cast spells. They passed notes to one another in a strange cryptic alphabet she elucidates in the journal. A is a briefcase. B is a cat face. None of it makes any sense. I am horrified.

"Mom, this is seriously, seriously uncool."

This only makes her laugh harder. Nana walks in the room to see us both on the floor. She offers to cut up some nutmallow, a Cleveland favorite, made of milk chocolate, walnuts, and marshmallow. We are all crazy for it. As we sit and chat, my grandmother takes my side.

"MIND was weird, Susan," she says to my mother. "You all wore black and skulked about looking unhappy and weird. That one kid, what was his name? He was almost definitely a little soft."

My grandmother has cut the nutmallow into perfect squares that sit on flowered china at the center of the table. She's also carved small wedges of cheese to put on crackers and placed it on a plate with salami, olives, and potato chips. A small bowl of onion dip sits directly to the right of the chips. It's a perfect Nana spread. I start to dig in, scooping and heaping dip on chips. Mom smiles at her mother and changes the subject. "Are you using that meditation pillow I bought you?" she asks.

Nana nods. "I am. It's great for my back. Helps me sit up straight."

"Yes, Mom, that's the best thing about it," my mother says. "Are you meditating?"

"Well, no. Not really. But one of these days."

I reach over to squeeze Nana's hand. I know how she feels. Meditation. Yoga. Gurus. MIND. I want her to know I am here for her. I wonder again how my grandmother, with her white pile carpet that looks brand-new, her impeccable antique couches, and her bright orange balls of spreadable cheeses could have produced my mother.

Just last week, I told my mother something important. "I have had every single cheerleader over to the house."

Jessica, Jill, and Kim have all sat on the sunporch off the dining room to drink cucumber water amid hundreds of plants and wicker furniture. I am so proud of having them here. Cheerleaders are the queen bees; we have watched movies in my dad's study, and they've waved to me at football games in their green and white short skirts and vests, their frosted hair sprayed and their lips painted pale pink shimmer, which makes them look more like corpses than a middle school dream.

We are still learning the ways of our developing bodies. We apply eyeliner with shaky hands and leave foundation streaks on our cheeks. We apply blush too liberally and often look vaudevillian as we sit in seventh-grade social studies, talking about the American Indians' impact on the land we now call home.

What I told my mother is correct. I have hung out with all the cheerleaders in the school, except one: Jessie Wyman. If I were a hunter, Jessie would be big game. If I were a thief, she'd be the big score. I am none of those things, but I am a wannabe popular girl, and no one is more popular than Donna Carey, an eighth-grade legend with hair that stands four inches high and breasts that bounce as she struts down the halls of our junior high. The boys call her "the Mighty DC" a legend who may or may not have been fingered in the local dollar cinema during a showing of *Dead Poet's Society*. She's definitely someone to know, but she's untouchable to all seventh graders, except Jessie, who is one of her best friends.

If I am ever going to get close to Donna, I need to go through Jessie, so I ask her to sleep at our house one Saturday night. *Ask* is kind of an oversimplification. I persist until finally she has enough and agrees. "But I can't come over until after practice and after I hang out with Donna," she says.

That's fine. I spend hours preparing the house. I set up the guest bedroom in the basement for us to sleep in. I move a TV and a VCR downstairs so we can watch movies. I fill the room with snacks—pretzels, popcorn, and chocolate bars—and I wait. She is supposed to arrive at six o'clock, and by one o'clock my stomach is hurting. By two o'clock I am vomiting. By four o'clock I am so dehydrated I can't even keep down the Gatorade my mother keeps pushing on me. Even water is impossible. I have a 102-degree fever.

"You've got a stomach bug," my mom says.

No! Not today!

My mother is logical. I know this. But she knows how important this is to me. She knows how much it took to get Jessie to come over. If I could get her to my house once, I know we would become best friends, and then I would be set socially.

I keep vomiting. I don't call. Jessie calls me at 5:30. My mother hands me the phone, mouthing the words "Tell her not to come." I shake my head. My throat is raw, the taste of vomit still fresh.

"So, I really want to hang out tonight with Donna and Jenny," says Jessie. "Can we do this another night?"

I put my hand over the phone to stifle the gagging as another wave of nausea and stomach pain seize my body. There would be no cancellation. I uncover the mouthpiece.

"I mean, you said yes. That is really rude," I say, trying to keep my voice steady. I am too sick to get mad, but even in my weakened state I am able to muster the passion to guilt-trip her. Despite my best efforts, Jessie, who is generally pretty smart and on top of her game, was on to me. "You don't sound good."

I roll my eyes just enough to bring on another wave of nausea. "I'm fine. If you don't come over, I will be really hurt and sad. You said you would."

I win. Two hours later—and ninety minutes late—she arrives.

"My mom and I just sat in front of your house with our mouths open. You really live here?" she asked, as she walked in the door.

We live on a high hill, and the ground lights make the house appear impressive, even from the outside at night. Windows span the entire living room, and the cathedral ceilings are really high. By Ohio standards the house makes us look rich, but I'd rather have her as a friend than be rich. That's how I will be really popular. It's not a John Hughes movie.

"Yep. We live here! Thanks for coming."

"You don't look so good," she tells me. "Can I make a call?"

She takes the cordless phone into another room, and I hear her calling Donna. A call placed to Donna from my house is really exciting. I try to listen from behind the door, but pretty soon I need to vomit again. Jessie comes out of the room, looking angry. "They are really having fun," she says, and I realize that Jessie is on tenuous ground, that her friendship with Donna, the Mighty DC, is as shaky as this sleepover is for me.

I crawl under the covers in the guest bed and fall asleep. When I wake up, my mother is in the playroom, sitting on the floor cross-legged and laughing, while Jessie turns cartwheels into splits.

"Now breathe," she tells Jessie in her yoga voice, something I had come to recognize as different from her normal voice—softer and more melodic, like a form of hypnosis.

Jessie presses her hands together in Anjali Mudra, her breath loud and clear.

"That's it," my mom says. "Now make the breath louder than any thought in your head."

I go back into the guest room to sleep. When I wake up, Jessie is gone. My mother doesn't say a word. She just covers me with a blanket and smiles.

"I'd offer you some Tylenol, but I don't think you'll be able to keep it down." She is right. I fall asleep, my head on fire with visions of Jessie and her crew at the movie theater, at McDonald's, and worst of all, at the football game, kissing high school boys by the concession stand, their jeans tight and revealing.

In the morning I feel better, albeit thirsty and weak. My mother hands me a note. The *i*'s are dotted with hearts, and the slanted hand-writing is perfect—obviously Jessie's. "I wish you had said you were sick. Your mom is cool. Glad I got to meet her. Feel better."

I look at my mom. Cool? No way. She gives me all her high school journals. "So you can see you are not alone in feeling alienated and weird."

"I don't feel alienated and weird," I tell her. I take the box of journals and read them one by one.

First Bra

I don't need a bra at all. It's more of a want thing. All the boys in fifth grade snap the girls' bra straps, and I don't want to be the only girl without a bra strap to snap. I tell my mother, and she gives me a look that it will take me twenty years to understand because it's only when my own ten-year-old daughter asks for her first bra that I will remember my mom's sigh of sadness.

"I don't think you need a bra," she says.

I insist. "I really need one. All the other girls have them."

"That's no reason to get one. You get one when you need it." She sighs. "You have your whole life for bras."

"I want one now."

This would work on my dad—rarely on her. But I have caught her in a weak mood. We head to the department store.

She buckles Mariel into her car seat, shoves some crackers in her pudgy little hand, and drives. The doors of the department store slide open, and we walk in and head straight to the back of the kids' section. There they are: rows of little bras. Lace ones. White ones. Beige ones. Pink lacy ones, with tiny cups and underwire.

"There are so many," I say in awe.

"I think we should stick with these training bras."

My hands instinctively go to my chest. For weeks I have been standing in front of the bathroom mirror, puffing my chest out, imagining that my tiny nipples are growing and that I have breasts. I have taken to wearing tight shirts so I can show off what little growth there is. Yet I am probably years away from actually needing a bra.

"What does 'training bra' mean? Is it training your body to grow boobs?"

My mother laughs. I wonder: *What is the training? Is this like boob boot camp? Will I be expected to do pull-ups and run a mile in this bra in less than ten minutes?*

She pulls one off the rack. It's white and lacy and has a pink bow right in the center. There is no underwire, which bums me out. I had been hoping for a really grown-up bra. This one looks like a glorified tank top. But it has a strap, and even though it's a pull-on bra, the bra strap can be pulled, and that's all I really want.

I go into the dressing room to try it on and admire myself in the mirror. There is something there. I am filling this bra out. Okay, so it's not even an A cup, but I am filling it—myself. No stuffing required.

"Mom! Mom! Come in here!"

"What's wrong? Are you okay?" She is standing outside the door, bouncing my little sister, who is only two. I open the door and let them both in.

"It looks good, right?" I do a turn. She gives me that look again. Right now I am reading it as victory.

"Is this really what you want?"

I nod my head so hard that I swear my brain is rattling in my skull. "Yes!"

"Take it off and I'll pay."

No. I want to wear it. I rip off the tags and hand them over. She takes them, looks at me, and tears up. "Okay. I'll pay."

I put my shirt on over my new bra and stare in the mirror. Finally.

Later at home, I am still wearing my new bra. My mother is downstairs in the kitchen with my sister. I go into my mother's room to find her journal. It's a green, well-worn spiral notebook. The top right corner is ripped off, and there is a coffee stain in the center of the cover, brown and sticky. I imagine her weeks ago, having her breakfast and placing a dripping mug on the journal. It's so her, this image, that I laugh to myself as I crouch in the small space between the bed and the wall. Downstairs, my sister screams, "Again! Again!" I know I am safe for now.

The last entry is two days ago. *She's growing up so fast. I am just glad I still have one baby.*

The writing blurs and I am crying, wiping the tears before they hit the page. I put the notebook down and promise myself not to read any more, but I know I am lying to myself. I will read it again in a few days.

My mother is a mystery I want to solve.

Experiments in Cooking Seaweed

My shorts are digging into my hips, and there is no breeze. Our house has central air-conditioning, but my mother isn't using it. All the windows are open, but the air is stagnant and feels oppressive.

"Can we please turn on the AC?" I whine.

"No," she says, for the fifth time. She read somewhere that air-conditioning messes with the immune system, and for a cancer patient a cold can be a serious problem. "We are letting the natural air inside."

And so we sweat. Summer in southern Ohio is notorious. Central air-conditioning is a standard feature of almost every house, and if my father were here instead of in Germany for two weeks, the house would be at sixty-five degrees and all would be well. But no. My mother is standing over a hot stove, water boiling, pulling apart sticky sheets of a green film I haven't seen before.

"What is that?" I ask, not because I want to know but because I am standing in the kitchen and feel obligated to converse.

"Seaweed."

Oh. Seaweed. Years from now I will get it. I will attend vegan sushi-making classes, but in landlocked Ohio, where the only fresh fish is trout, these sheets of green paper look nothing like food.

"What are you going to do with it?" I ask. My only experience with seaweed is seeing it wash up on the shore during our summer vacations in South Carolina, on Cape Cod, or in Rhode Island. I imagine this food on the sand, surrounded by flies that are buzzing and regurgitating all over the rotting flesh.

"I am going to wrap it around brown rice."

She points to the pot simmering with water. It has boiled over at least twice so far, and foamy white stuff drips down the sides and covers the burner underneath the pot. My mother keeps fidgeting with the knobs to turn down the heat, but she becomes impatient and turns it up again.

She is also broiling carrots. No wonder it's a thousand degrees in our kitchen. The tile beneath my feet is the only cool part of the house. Even the natural wood cabinets look shiny and slick with sweat.

"It's macrobiotic," my mother says.

I immediately understand. Last week she spent a few days at the home of my father's friend's wife, Yvonne. She's a cancer survivor and a macrobiotic cook. Although I know my mother has breast cancer and she is being treated, my parents keep most of the details from me. What I do know is that she's chosen a less rigorous path of treatment, including altering her diet, practicing more yoga, and doing meditation.

As far as I can tell, macrobiotic just means bland. Bland and vegan. No meat. No dairy. No sugar. No Bueno.

A few years later, after my mother is gone, Gwyneth Paltrow will become famous and tout the many benefits of her own macrobiotic diet, and this whole grain, veggie-heavy lifestyle will enjoy a brief, highly faddish moment in the sun. But in 1990 this diet is the final insult after spending most of my childhood being denied Lucky Charms, Pudding Pops, and Kool-Aid.

I watch as my mother carefully steams the seaweed and drains the rice. Perfect sushi rice is both sticky and fluffy. It holds together by itself and offers a perfect chewy bite. This rice does none of that. Some of the long grains are burnt and crunchy.

I watch my mother chop the carrots and attempt to ball up the rice. She's cursing because the carrots are still too stiff, and none of this is how she learned it in her cooking lesson. She's undeterred. She tosses the rice and starts a new pot of water to boil. The water sizzles as it hits the pan, and the room is sweltering.

Guilt Trips over Yoga

"Leaving again?" I ask. "For two weeks?" I roll my eyes so hard they seem to hit my brow bone. Then I stop, glaring at my mother the way only a preteen can. "Weren't you just gone for two weeks?"

My mother is in yoga teacher training in a program at the Kripalu Center in Lenox, Massachusetts, where she goes three times a year for a two-week retreat. She's been going for as long as I remember, but these retreats seem to be coming fast and furious, and twelve-year-old me is pissed.

"This is how the training works, honey. If I could do it any other time, I would, but I can't. It's the program."

I roll my eyes again and slump lower in my seat, crossing my skinny arms across the front of my body so hard that the bones of my wrists dig into my ribs. If *harrumph* were an actual thing people said, I am pretty sure I would have said it.

We are in the car on our way to Knoxville, Tennessee, to visit my mother's sister. My mother fiddles with the radio and smiles. "Time in a Bottle" by Jim Croce is playing. "What a perfect song for this moment," she says, singing along with the lyrics—off-pitch, of course. Normally this would make me smile, but not today.

> *If I could make days last forever*
> *If words could make wishes come true*
> *I'd save every day like a treasure and then,*
> *Again, I would spend them with you.*
> *But there never seems to be enough time*
> *To do the things you want to do*
> *Once you find them.*
> *I've looked around enough to know*
> *That you're the one I want to go*
> *Through time with.*

I know the song. My mother plays it on her guitar all the time, and I can sing along with her. In the backseat, from her 1980s-issue car seat with a giant bar across the front, my four-year-old sister pipes in. "Time in a bo-o-ottle, bo-o-ottle, mottle."

This makes me smile, but I am still angry.

Outside the car, kudzu climbs up rolling hills, the first sign that we have crossed from Kentucky into Tennessee. I watch it go by at warp speed, the rich green blurring through my tears. *She's always gone. This yoga thing matters more to her than we do.*

I look back at my sister, and she's smiling. Her face is covered with chocolate from a Hershey bar. She'd taken the wrapper off, thrown it on the floor, and held the squares of chocolate between her palms until they grew squishy. Then she licked the chocolate off her palms, spreading the rest over her face in a thin layer.

"She's so gross," I tell my mother, who just smiles. This is the kind of thing my mother can take. At home, unless our cleaning lady has been there, our carpet is covered in crumbs. The counters in our kitchen are eternally sticky, and stains on the couch remain for weeks.

When I was a couple of years younger, my father was driving me from Dayton to Columbus with his secretary in the front seat. She put some jelly on toast to hand back to me and somehow managed to smash the jam-covered bread into the ceiling of the car. I look up and see that the red stain is still there, more than three years later.

This is my mom. Later I will learn this is also yoga. Nonattachment. If *samadhi* (enlightenment) is the last part of the eight-limbed path of the yogi, then *aparigraha* (nonattachment) is the wisdom that comes with it.

Sitting in a car, driving through Appalachia, I am not thinking of the yamas (the moral, ethical, and societal guidelines for the practicing yogi*)*. But maybe my mother is. Maybe she is looking at me, her preteen daughter full of attachment and anger and selfishness, and she is modeling the behavior she hopes she will one day see in me.

We own nothing. We own no one. We are not attached to cars, money, fame, or politics. But no prepubescent girl in the world is thinking this, and especially not me. Not now. I am angry. My mother is leaving again, and my father spends all his time going to Germany, Japan, Thailand, and Brazil. My father is never home, and now my mother is never home, either.

I slump lower in my seat. I need my mom. I need to tell her what happened at school. She knows all my friends and knows which ones to call creeps and cretins, who is going out with whom, who has a crush on what boy, and what teacher is mean. My mother strokes my hair late at night when I can't sleep and I am crying because Nicky Brown, the meanest girl in seventh grade, is writing offensive things on my locker and whispering mean things about me to my best friends.

My mother knows none of this because I don't tell her. I am silent. Eventually she turns off the radio. In the silence between us, I wonder what she is thinking—maybe about her practice and how it makes her feel when her feet are rooted into the earth in the Tadasana (mountain) pose, palms facing forward, ready for anything, the crown of her head lifting toward the sky. The energy in our bodies is always moving in two directions, rooting us down and lifting us up at the same time. Or maybe she is thinking of Shirshasana (headstand), when the blood rushes into her head and everything feels focused and clear.

Maybe she isn't thinking of yoga at all. There is a secret between us, something she isn't sharing with anyone else. Last week she found a hard lump in her breast, like a small stone just to the left of her nipple. Her doctor told her to wait a bit to see if it grows. This advice will turn out to be a death sentence, but she doesn't know this now. We don't know that our time is slipping away and that the lump means the end.

In that car that day, she thinks we have decades before we will be parted for good. What difference does two weeks here and there matter? Would she have changed anything if she knew? If sharing the magic of yoga and the eight-limbed path was her calling and her mission, maybe it was more important than spending half of March with her kids.

"You know this is something I just need to do. Maybe someday you will understand."

I doubt it!

My mind has already shifted. I am thinking of my cousin's pool, of the projects my aunt always has for us, of the fun restaurant where you fish for your own food, and of the barbecue that puts anything else in southern Ohio to shame.

"Turn the radio back on," I tell her. "But none of that whiny folk. I want something better."

A Week at Kripalu

I am meeting my mother at Kripalu after spending a week in New York City with my uncles. It's the first time they have given me any freedom in the city, and my friend Amy (who came along) and I took cabs to museums and walked to Central Park. We flirted with the boy who lived in my uncles' building and told cabbies, with aplomb, to drive to 79th and Riverside. For two girls from Ohio, this was pretty damn sophisticated, and my mother wondered aloud about it on the phone.

"How am I going to keep you down on the farm after you've seen New York this way?"

I laughed. But it was true. I was sure that as soon as I got to New York City (which I would do as soon as I graduated from high school), all would be right in the world. This is also the first trip where I have become aware of sexiness. As I am walking down the street in my tight jean shorts and fitted white top, a man stops in front of me. "I wish I was them blue jeans," he said.

I misheard him. "You wish you had blue jeans?" I asked. Amy gave

82

me a hard shove and told me to keep walking.

My uncles took us out for ice cream one night and screamed at a man who kept staring. "She's sixteen, you fucking pervert!"

I couldn't quite figure it out. My breasts had finally shown up a few months before the trip, and I went from a B cup to a D (and climbing) within a few weeks. I'd wished and prayed and hoped to fill a bra, and now that I did, it was like having two strange new appendages. I wasn't quite sure what to do with them, which is a lot of the reason I spent the summer at the pool hiding under a bulky sweatshirt. But New York was hot and sticky in August, and I'd bought new clothing I wanted to show off for the trip. The attention was new and exciting, and I couldn't wait to tell my mom about it.

I knew my mother was sexy. I never would have used that word, but my whole life I had noticed the way men looked at her, and more than one man had told me how beautiful she was. I wanted to be like her. I wanted to have the same effect on men. She never wore high heels, makeup, or low-cut necklines. She never painted her lips red or even dyed her hair. Her sexiness was in her blood. It was the way she moved her knees when she watched TV and threw her head back when she laughed. It was innate, and I wanted to be just like her—body, mind, and soul.

But I was a disappointment.

"Why don't you date?" She asked me that one Saturday afternoon, a few months before the New York trip and the day after all the athletic teams wore their uniforms to school. I'd worn my tennis uniform and caught the eye of a boy in the school, who called to ask me out.

"You just looked good in your skirt, and I want to get to know you," he told me. My mother had answered and was standing in the dining room with her thumbs up.

"It's a boy," she mouthed.

I listened to him make his pitch. I'd never met him, but it didn't matter. "You just looked good in your skirt" wasn't doing it for me.

"Do you make a habit of calling girls and telling them you think they are hot?"

My mother looked as though she wanted to cry. Once I hung up, she asked me why I had said no.

"Would you date someone who knew nothing about you and only wanted to date you because of your skirt?"

She laughed and agreed, but I could tell that she thought my lack of interest in boys was suspect, which is why she would have been happy to see me in New York—flirting, laughing, and noticing the way men looked at me and not wanting to smack them for it. I had turned sixteen two weeks ago.

My mother had three months to live. But none of us knew that.

I fly from LaGuardia Airport to Boston, where a car meets me and drives me to Kripalu. Summer in the Berkshires is a dreamy time, when people come from around the country to Tanglewood, an outdoor music festival that hosts James Taylor, symphony orchestras, and other musical performances. Kripalu is in Lenox, which really should be the first photo that comes up when you Google "quaint New England towns." In the fall it lights up with orange, red, and yellow foliage that draws tourists from all around. It's also home to two wellness centers: Canyon Ranch, a high-end spa frequented by celebrities and rich people, and Kripalu.

As we pass Canyon Ranch, I look out the window. Why can't my mother take us there instead? I imagine massages, pedicures, and manicures—something far cushier than what I see as we pull up the long drive toward Kripalu, sitting on top of a hill, surrounded by lush trees with a massive lawn that goes on for thousands of feet. During the day people bring their meals there to sit quietly while they eat. The building looks austere, institutional. My mother tells me it was once a convent, which seems about right. It's red brick, which makes it look more like a school than a place of spiritual enlightenment.

At the bottom of the lawn, a path leads to a small lake with a sandy beach and opportunities to kayak or go out in a paddleboat. Bikes in the shed are available to the guests.

As the car pulls up, my mother and sister run out to greet me. My mother is dressed all in white, and I cringe at her hairy ankles and giant glasses. A week in New York made me especially fashion-conscious, and she is not fashionable. She hugs me tight, tips the driver, and offers to take Mariel and me for a walk. My sister is ornery. She'd rather go back to the room and nap, so my mother leads me inside. I have been in the building before, but I have never stayed here. It smells like clean laundry and tofu, and I am sure I will not enjoy a second of this stay.

We head straight to the room, which is the opposite of cushy. The walls are painted a generic tan, and the carpet is institutional, nothing like the hotels I have grown up staying in with my dad, like the Intercontinental in Paris just a few months ago. Compared to that, Kripalu looks a little like a low-security prison. But the sheets are clean and the room is cool, thanks to an overhead fan.

We are alone in the room, just the three of us, which I will later learn is unusual for Kripalu. Most people stay in dorms that sleep up to a dozen people. We have a double bed and a cot. My sister and my mother have already stayed one night, and they are sleeping in the double bed, which leaves me with the cot. I am cool with that. My mother hands me a wool blanket "just in case."

I plop all my things onto the bed and look at my mother. "This place is awful. I can't stay here." My eyes well up. My voice sounds loud to me, as though everyone on the floor can hear me, and the thought of seven days in this quiet, sterile environment where the whipped cream is made of cashews is almost more than I can bear.

My mom is pissed. "Suck it up, Sasha. This is a gift, so try to enjoy it."

I want the familiar. I want luxury and comfort and a room of my own. I want food I recognize and voices that are allowed to climb above a whisper. It doesn't occur to me that this is an opportunity or that I should be grateful. It doesn't occur to me that my mother is sharing something that means a lot to her and that it will be the last time she can do so. The only thing that occurs to me is that I am uncomfortable and I want her to be, too.

But I also know I have no choice. I sigh. I heave myself onto the bed and turn on my side, feeling the tears come. It's not just about Kripalu. I miss Amy and my uncles' apartment. I miss the freedom of the city.

I hear my mother and my sister leave the room, so I turn to look up at the ceiling. One week. One week. One week.

The program my mother and I are enrolled in is called Transformation through Transition. My sister is in the kids' camp, which seems to be pretty much like a summer camp. They go horseback riding and roast bananas over a fire. They watch movies and run on the lawn. I watch her go off with the other little kids after dinner and wish I could follow. Instead I join my mother in one of the big rooms, and we sit in a circle in order to "share." This doesn't sound good.

I am the youngest by many decades, which makes me a source of excitement and kindness. Everyone wants to know my story, and they gather around, telling me how brave I am for being here. This makes me nervous. I don't consider my participation brave. Why should it be? What am I in for?

As we begin to share, I get an idea. This program is about emotional catharsis, which appears to be what happens when you have forty or so years of bottled-up emotions and you come here to release them. I do not have forty years of emotions. I barely have sixteen.

We break into small groups. Everyone is there for a different reason. My mother and I choose not to be in a group together. No one else in our program knows each other, so it just makes sense. When we sit down, we start to do some kind of regression, per our leader's instructions. One person plays the mom of the group of four women, and one person plays the child. I am chosen as the mom by every woman.

"Something about you just feels so maternal," says a woman who is at least forty-five years older than I am. She puts her head in my lap and sobs. I run my fingers through her hair in an attempt to soothe, but I am unnerved.

"*Shh . . . shh.*"

I think of my father and how in six days he will fly into Boston from his business trip in London and drive here to see us. Then we will all go back to Ohio. I tell myself to remember that he will come, and all will be well, calm, and normal. Just six days.

Then it's my turn. I randomly choose a woman named Marcie. I don't choose her because of her energy, but because she looks a little like my mom. She's about her age, and she seems like the least emotional of the bunch.

We are supposed to start with a hug, so I reach out and pull her into an awkward embrace. I am generally not a hugger. I have to know someone really well to want their whole person smashed against me, and I do not know this woman at all. Nevertheless, we hug. She tears up. Oh shit.

"I am not a crier," I tell her. But it's not true. I cry all the time. I just don't do it in front of people. That feels weak. I feel an expectation to perform emotion. That is, if I don't cry and show catharsis, I will be the weirdo. But what am I sad about?

Suddenly my heart is pounding. "My mom is sick."

They reach for my hands.

Well, you are all the same age. I'm thinking. *Why can't it be you instead?* I don't say that, of course. Instead I tell them how hard it's been, that I think people are lying to me, and that I am scared she won't get better. Then I cry because the things I am saying are true. I am scared, and I've been keeping it in all summer. Maybe all year. Maybe for the past five years.

We've been living our lives as though everything is normal. But my mom is not well. People keep telling us that "you'll be laughing about this in a year." They keep saying that once she is in remission again, all will be well. But it's a lie. On some level I already know that. No one is laughing, and the news keeps getting worse.

I don't know these women. I think of a movie I saw recently with my mother, *St. Elmo's Fire*, which tells the story of five college friends and all the drama that real life brings.

"These people are dreadful," Mom said. They really were. We laughed throughout the movie, and I teased her later about a dreadful comment when Demi Moore tries to kill herself and Rob Lowe gives some dramatic speech about the fire. "I never thought I'd be so tired at twenty-two," Moore says.

It seems appropriate now at Kripalu. "I never thought I'd be so tired at sixteen," I say.

It's easier to feel movie emotions, so I cry into the lap of a stranger. Everyone comforts me, pats my head, and tells me I will be okay. I've already shut down enough that I only half believe them.

Nothing is going to be okay.

Later that night, as I go to bed, my mother is still awake. "Did you like any of that or did you just completely hate it?" she asks.

"It was okay, Mom. I don't know. I just feel like it's weird to cry in a room with a bunch of strangers."

"It's supposed to be a release, a way to clear the mind and the body of old, stale energy, so you can work better within the light. It's a yoga thing."

She laughs, but I can tell she's not relaxed. She's in some pain. She reaches for a bottle of Tylenol and takes one with a sip of water. I watch her do this and wonder about the pain. Is it the cancer? Or is she sore from all the yoga and walking?

I want to ask her. I want to hug her. I want her to be my mom in the group, and I want to tell her I'm scared. But there is a line with my mom, and I know that bringing up the truth would cross it. I tell her I'm fine, that I like everyone and that the program will be okay.

"It's a lot to ask," she says, staring ahead in the dark. I see her profile, and I'm not sure she's talking to me, but I answer anyway.

"What? What's a lot to ask?"

"This. All of it. It's a lot to ask of us all."

The Tylenol must kick in because she settles down in bed and turns on her side, her back to me. I listen as her breathing becomes heavier. My sister's snoring and Mom's heavy breathing make it hard to fall asleep, so I pull a pillow over my head and try to muffle the sounds.

"I'm in hell," I whisper into the dark. This is the worst thing that could happen. I am stuck here on catharsis island, with a hippie and a rambunctious child, and their snoring and ragged breathing are the two worst things in the world.

At sixteen, I find this too much to ask. My mother is right. It's too much to ask me to know what's really going on: that this is the last time we will have a week like this, that things will get much worse, and that the glimpse of reality I had in that session will become our full-time reality in just a few weeks. For now I am a kid, and it is too much to ask.

Yoga classes are offered twice a day. I don't know enough about the practice to choose a level, and my mother's pain is obvious, even to a self-absorbed teenager. She is limping and has to go back to the room every afternoon to take a long rest. But we always make it to early-morning practice. She chooses gentle yoga, and since I don't know the difference I tag along. It's the kind of yoga my mother always does.

We draw the breath in. We hold it there. We feel it in our lungs and we exhale. We do this again and again. In my mind it seems like half an hour, but it may be shorter. Eventually we enter the Child pose and hold, breathing the same way. We follow these gentle movements, ending with a supported shoulder stand and Savasana (final rest).

My mind is racing the whole time. I left my sneakers at home, but I wish I had them now because I can feel my fingers start to fidget and my toes wiggle. I need to release energy. My mother would tell me that's exactly why I need to relax into the practice, but it's much harder than it should be. Sometimes you just need to run.

Everyone else looks relaxed. My mother is on her side in Savasana. I watch her left rib cage rise and fall with every breath, and I synchronize my breathing with hers.

My fingers stop moving. My toes let go. My heart rate slows. I keep my eyes open, soothed by the rise and fall, and I think that maybe this is how it was when I was in her belly, when the only sounds I heard were her heartbeat, her blood, and the small layer of water between me and her skin.

I feel this sensation again five years later, when I am in college and take a scuba diving class. We train for months before the first dive. We fall backward in the university pool and sit at the bottom of the deep end, breathing through our mouthpieces and grinning like idiots. But when it comes time to take the first dive in the frigid waters off the coast of Ogunquit, Maine, I balk.

We swim in one line, our teacher at the front and her assistant at the back. Five of us will descend one by one. As soon as I am three feet under, I become disoriented and afraid. There isn't much to see in the Maine ocean in the middle of March, but the strands of red kelp swaying around us start to look sinister, and the rocks at the bottom appear jagged and dangerous. Every foot we descend makes my heart race faster. I want to be on the surface, to breathe air. My breath is jagged and panicked, and my gloved hands start to shake against the water.

I remember that moment as I am practicing with my mother. I remember the rise and fall of her breath. I imagine that the water around me is amniotic fluid, and I tell myself again and again, *You are safe. You are safe.* Things shift and change. The rocks look smoother. The kelp looks pretty and in union with my breath. The water feels supportive and buoyant instead of something that is closing in around me. I am fully present back in the womb. I am safe.

That moment, five years from now, is born during my practice at Kripalu. I close my eyes and let go.

"My bones hurt," my mother says, as we make our way toward the cafeteria for breakfast. I want to ask her if that's a bad sign, if it means the cancer drugs aren't working. But I don't ask because I don't want to scare her and also because maybe I don't want to know.

My sister has a meltdown because there is too much cinnamon in the oatmeal, and she doesn't like it that way. Breakfast is supposed to be silent, so my mother shuttles Mariel out, shushing her loudly and generally making a scene, while I stay to eat my breakfast in peace. But the quiet breakfast isn't peaceful for me. I hear everything: the clattering of forks, the knives cutting into meatless sausage, the cracking of hard-boiled eggs, and the tapping of feet on the linoleum floor.

I dunk my ginger tea bag again and again and again. The women behind me are whispering, and some from our group smile and wave, but they are quickly shushed by one of the meandering attendants.

I wonder what might happen if I screamed and jumped on top of the table—wiggling, yelling, dancing, and shouting—but I already know the answer. I would be gently guided down and told about the many energy-releasing offerings that start around noon. I leave the dining hall and pass a room with an altar and many flowers around it. Gurudev is in the house, or at least he will be later in the day. I wander to our room and find my mother on the bed, facedown.

"Are you coming to the session?"

She shakes her head and rolls over. The pillow has wet spots, and I can tell she's been crying. "I'm not up to it, okay? Go without me."

I stand in the doorway, watching her. I don't want to go to the session without her. I am here to go with her. Even if we don't spend the time together, I like knowing she's in the room. I feel safer knowing she's close. I tell her none of this, however.

"Mom, that's ridiculous. Get up. You paid for it. What a waste of money."

Through gritted teeth, she sits up slowly and with great effort. "I don't care about the money. I don't feel well. Go without me. And shut the door on your way out."

I do what she asks and make my way down to our morning session, which is just getting started.

"Where is your mom?" Marcie asks when she sees me walk in alone.

"She's upstairs. Upset stomach."

I lie because I remember that they caught the cancer early and she's fine, and I don't want to have to explain all of that to Marcie or anyone else. I can tell she knows otherwise, though, by the way she looks at me with a mix of pity and concern. Her eyebrows knit together, and I want to smack her.

"Do you want to talk about it?" she asks, holding out her hands.

Definitely not. I don't have to answer because our leader walks in just then and announces that we will be painting our feelings outside today. Great. That sounds horrible.

But it's not. I am partnered with a woman named Maggie, who lives in Boston. Actually she lives in Belmont, which sounds like a pretty suburb of Boston, from the way she describes it.

"It's all brick houses and pretty lawns," she says with a laugh, and I imagine all of Boston to be impossibly sophisticated—like New York, but smarter and a little more well-heeled. Maggie has two sons, both a bit older than I am. I figure she could use some "girl" time, and I could definitely use some "mom" time. We talk the whole time I am painting. I am not an artist, and I spend a lot of time being envious of people who are. But today I just focus on the moment, on my brush dipped in water, on the way it picks up the colors and spreads them onto paper. The colors represent my feelings.

At first I try to paint a cat because I love cats and it seems simple enough. But the watercolors are impossible to control, and soon my pink and purple cat morphs into some kind of strange sea creature with a hump and wisps of purple and pink bands all around its tail. Then that creature changes as the paper soaks through and the colors blend. I laugh. So does Maggie. She is making a wheelbarrow, and hers is perfectly recognizable, which I admire.

"I totally see it!" I tell her. "But why a wheelbarrow?"

"To carry it all away," she says.

I wonder what she needs to carry away. She's divorced, but I don't know much else about her. "I'm not a yogi," she says.

This immediately makes me more comfortable. "I'm not either," I reply, laughing. Even though we are about thirty years apart in age, she is a kindred spirit, another person wondering what the hell she is doing in this strange land of hippies in flowing linen.

"Yours looks like you cried all over it," Maggie says, pointing to the pools of water and the streaks of color running up the edges of the paper. She's right. Maybe I did. The cat I tried to make became something else, and then it became nothing more than a soggy mess.

"You can try again," she says.

But we aren't supposed to. We are supposed to look at our creations and figure out what they mean. Mine looks messy, uncomfortable, sloppy, and wrong. I put it on the drying rack anyway, and we walk inside to do our meditation.

"Sit with your breath," our leader says, and when I open my eyes I see Maggie has her eyes open, too, and she winks at me. I smile and close my eyes, feeling safer now. I can see my third eye. I keep thinking of the painting, the way my plan morphed and eventually looked nothing like a cat or any kind of animal in the living world. I think about my mother back in the room and how she missed the painting, and I am guessing she wouldn't have enjoyed it, anyway. She's not really crafty. But her absence feels wrong, as though something is missing, and I can't quite get fully comfortable here.

I focus on the beam of light between my eyebrows. I use my breath to make it grow brighter and stronger, more electric. I see colors blending, merging, bleeding together. The light grows bigger and spreads from my third eye all the way up my forehead, filling my skull, but even then I can't erase all the thoughts filling my head. They start pooling, like the water on my painting. Will my mother be okay? Is she sicker than she is telling us? There is a truth there. I know there is, but I am afraid to name it. I am afraid to say what it is because when I do, I won't ever be able to change it.

She's dying.

I think it, then I shut it down. I open my eyes and shake it off. I look at the clock. It's 11:45 AM. We are just in time for yoga dance, and I need it.

I drag Maggie with me. "I promise, the first time I took it I thought it was totally weird, too," I tell her. The class is free-form, with drummers sitting in a circle. It's my favorite class at the ashram. The drummers play beats, and we just let loose, moving our bodies in whatever way feels good. Sometimes there are games in which we stand in a circle and copy one another's movements, but by the end of the hour everyone is moving to her own rhythm and living the dance.

Later I ask why it's called yoga dance, and the lead drummer explains that it's "giving your body permission to move in the way that feels good." I nod, but that's not how I have experienced yoga. When my mother practices, it's quiet. It's more about the breath and the mindfulness than any movement. There is no cardio element. When she does move, it's in slow poses for five to ten breaths, opening more, breathing more, shifting her gaze. It's torturous.

This, however, is joyful. Magic. This is heart-pounding, foot-tapping magic. But I see what he means. If this is yoga, maybe yoga isn't so bad.

The next day my mother comes with me to yoga dance, but she sits on the side. Her breathing is labored, and I realize later she's there because I love it. I try to pull her into the circle, but she stays seated. Mariel joins me, and we hop around and shimmy our shoulders. I pick her up and swing her around, and all three of us laugh. Maggie is there, too, and she pulls my sister around. The three of us move in and out of poses, jumps, and kicks.

My mother is smiling, but her eyes are full of tears. I stop dancing and watch her watching Maggie and Mariel. I pull Mariel's hand. "Come on, let's go back to the room."

"Why? I'm having fun," Mariel says, twirling on her bare feet and making her long brown hair twirl with her. Her feet are dirty from spending all day outside, and she's as close to feral as she's ever been. But she's happy.

"We just need to go," I say, pointing toward our mom. I wish Mariel was older so I could explain it in a better way. But she's not. She's only seven. I do the best I can with what I have, and I yank her hard by the arm.

"Ow," she yells, glaring at me and then at my mom. "Sasha pulled my arm."

"Sasha, don't pull her arm." She heaves a heavy sigh and asks me to help her up, which I do. "I need to go back to the room."

"I'll go with you," I tell her, and even though she tells us not to, I can tell she's glad we come with her. We all get into the beds, and even though it's only one o'clock in the afternoon, we fall asleep.

An hour later my mother wakes us up. The second part of our program is coming up, and she is determined to make it.

"Get up, Sasha, we need to go." She's shaking me, and it's annoying, but her energy is good to see. I jump up to greet her.

The session runs long, and dinner is a blur of tempeh, roasted broccoli, and various foods I am not interested in trying. Tempeh is like tofu, only much more disgusting. At least this is what I tell my mother. "It's foul and I won't touch it."

There are no other choices, though, and eventually my hunger wins out. I put the tough soy product on a fork and try to chew it. I gag each time my teeth close. *This is a nightmare.* Each bite is misery, but I choke it down. It's not even dessert night, either.

"I will never eat that again."

"Okay, Sasha. Never again."

She's on to other things. Tonight she is "definitely, almost surely going to get Mariel into a shower." I'll believe it when I see it. She's been saying it for the past few days. But it does seem like Mariel has reached a critical mass of dirt that can no longer be covered over by some hand soap or pretended away with some yoga breath. It's time.

Back in the room Mariel strips down, but before she heads to the shower, she starts yoga dancing. It's like some primitive precursor to twerking, and seeing a naked, dirty seven-year-old with a mushroom haircut like this sends my mother and I into hysterical laughter. We are doubled over, tears streaming down our faces, laughing so much it only encourages my sister, who slinks across the floor. "Butt dance! Butt dance!"

We can't stop laughing. My mom throws a towel over my sister, but that doesn't stop her from butt dancing her way down the hall and through the shower. The communal bathrooms with their pink tile have never witnessed anything quite so loud and raucous. Everyone who walks in looks askance, which makes us giggle harder.

By the time we go to bed, we are exhausted. Mariel falls asleep first, and my mom is reading a Dick Francis novel.

"Do you think the doctors are right?" I whisper. "Do you think you'll be okay?"

"Yes," my mom says, sliding a bookmark into her book. But she doesn't look at me. "There are no guarantees, honey. All we have is now. Today. This moment. This breath."

"Tell me the truth," I plead.

"The truth is, I might get hit by a bus tomorrow morning."

That goddamn bus. People are always referencing it. Of course it's true. Any one of us could be hit by a bus, a truck, a flower cart, or even a tractor. We could be crushed by a piano falling from above or a piece of luggage falling from a plane. There are a million ways to die; I know this, and she knows this, and we are all just living our lives, inching our way toward death. But she knows what I mean, and I want the truth.

"Sasha, it is the truth. No one knows. I can't promise you a thing. But if I didn't have cancer, I couldn't promise you anything then, either. All we have is now."

I am tired. For tonight, it's enough. I smile. "Now is good, Mom. Today was good. It was a good, good day."

"The best," Mom agrees. She shuts off her light.

A good day. It is the last time I will ever see her laugh that way again, the last time the three of us will dance and sing and do the butt dance. But as we both settle down in our beds and let ourselves drift off, we have no idea. The peace of the present moment is all we have. For that, we are lucky. We are alive. We are present.

By the time my dad arrives, we have an established routine. Wake up. Go to early morning yoga and meditation. Eat breakfast. Go to our morning program. Go to yoga dance. Eat lunch. Go to the afternoon program. Eat dinner. Sleep. Repeat. I still don't like the food. Tempeh makes me want to throw up. I miss steak and french fries. I miss barbecued chicken and macaroni with real cheese.

We see Gurudev on Wednesday night. I learn that the altar with flowers is always there, waiting for him. This week he came just once, to give his talk. Much like he was when we saw him in Ohio, he enters with bare feet and a simple robe. But this time it feels less moving. We are on his turf, in his space, right near his parking space.

Maybe the spell has broken for me, but not for my mom. She watches him. She bows toward him. She joins the line of people waiting to touch his feet.

My father arrives by cab around four o'clock in the afternoon. He had called from a pay phone in Lenox, so we know he is close and run to the lobby to greet him. He ambles through the sliding front doors, suit bag slung over his shoulder, a good seventy pounds heavier than any man we'd seen for the last six days.

He smirks. "I see Gurudev still has his parking spot."

My mother rolls her eyes and kisses him on the cheek. He's going to spend one night here with us, and when our program ends tomorrow afternoon, we will all head home. I am sad, not ready to leave this place. But seeing my father means other things, too: ribs. Ice cream. Real sugar.

"So do I get to bust you guys out of here?" he asks.

My mother and my sister are walking ahead of us, and I am telling him about my week.

"Sounds like you guys cried a lot. Did you get to see the exalted guru?"

I laugh. "Oh, Gurudev," I say. "Barefoot wonder with parking spaces a-plenty, tell us how to live, O wise one."

I think of my mother touching his feet, of the people in the room with their heads bowed toward him. I think of the little bit I can remember from his talk, and I feel wrong making fun of him. But I don't stop.

"He's kind of sleazy," I tell my dad.

"That's what I think."

We get to the room, and my mom opens the door. My dad feigns happiness, but I can tell this simple room is not what he had in mind after six hours on a plane.

"Where are we going to eat?"

Mom stays at the ashram while Dad takes us into town. Lenox is upscale and quaint, full of expensive stores catering to people from Manhattan and Boston. Stores with handmade signs and home-churned ice cream dot the New England landscape, and they make a lot of money during tourist season.

It's been a week since I've had real dairy. Kripalu offers clotted cashew cream to put on top of strawberry shortcake—no ice cream. I order a double scoop of mint chocolate chip and chocolate peanut butter. My sister orders chocolate in a cup with rainbow sprinkles. We smile at each other. The ice cream is smooth. The mint makes my whole tongue light up, and I close my eyes just to feel it.

This is mindful eating, as we learned at Kripalu, the art of doing nothing else as you eat. Savor each bite. Taste it all. Memorize the textures and flavors and all the sensations that arise as you nourish and hydrate the body.

I savor only the first bite. The rest I gulp down loudly, chewing my cone into little bits and finishing long before Mariel and Dad.

Then we go out for ribs and french fries. It's perfect.

The next day we leave the ashram. I hug Maggie and all the women in the program. I am relieved to go home, to have one last week of summer and gallons of ice cream in the freezer.

I will miss this place, though. I wonder if I will ever return.

"Of course you will," my mother promises, as Kripalu fades in the distance and we head toward the highway. "I go multiple times a year. You will come with me."

She's right. We will come back next year to plant a tree in her memory; and the year after, when they dedicate it. Then each time my grandparents come to visit us in Boston, we will go to see her tree.

One day the tree will be gone. No one will know what happened to it, but we will keep going anyway—to eat tempeh and chew it mindfully, to practice that slow-burning Kripalu yoga and meditate for hours every day.

But we know none of this now. My mother turns to me from the front of the car. "I am proud of you. You did really well. You made me more social than I've ever been there."

"Social?" I laugh. "You?"

She turns around and shuts her eyes. She sleeps most of the way to the airport.

4. Saluting

WE SALUTE THE SUN IN A TRADITIONAL WAY.
ALMOST EVERY YOGA CLASS BEGINS AND
ENDS WITH A SUN SALUTATION,
STARTING AT THE TOP OF THE MAT AND MOVING
THROUGH A STRENGTH-BUILDING CHATURANGA
(BOTTOM OF A PUSH-UP) INCLUDING A BACK BEND,
AND ENDING WITH HOME BASE (DOWNWARD DOG).
OUR GOAL IS TO WARM UP THE SPINE.

SUN B WARMS UP THE HIPS.
IT IS A LITTLE MORE VIGOROUS AND
INCLUDES WARRIOR ONE
AND A CHAIR POSE AT THE TOP OF THE MAT.

Guinea Pig Death No. 1

My family is in Hawaii when the guinea pigs die. I am eight. We have leis around our necks as we step off the plane, and the smell of hibiscus is in the air. My mother is pregnant with my sister. My father drives us along mountain roads, gripping the wheel so tight his knuckles turn white. One night, in our Maui hotel, my mother and father have a screaming match so loud it wakes the people next door. The next day we have two breakfasts, two sets of macadamia nut pancakes: one with my fuming mother, her hands shaking with rage, and another with my father, who joked and acted silly through slitted eyes. Later we take a long walk around the hotel grounds while my parents make up alone in the room.

Green is what I remember. Green vines. Green grass. Green moss on every tree. Life bursts from every seam in Hawaii. Flowers refuse to stay budded and tight. They burst forth, their petals colorful and wide. In Hawaii the conditions are so ripe that life must be constantly beaten back. Every morning the sand is swept from every surface near the beach. Seaweed carts are piled high with anything that washed up during the night.

The grass is cut, the weeds are whacked. The space between each slat of wood on every deck must be picked clean as the plants twist and writhe and try to find the light. My mother must have gotten the call, but no one tells me.

I don't find out until we get home, bleary-eyed and buzzed from fifteen hours in a plane and a six-hour time difference. "Let's get them," I say, referring to Karen and Brian, my best friends—my guinea pigs. They have spent the week with our neighbors, Sarah's family. There's still enough light. It isn't too late to get them tonight. I've been nervous. Sarah's kids are rough; they have gone through rabbits and dogs and all manner of reptiles.

"Are you sure they're the right people?" I ask my parents before we leave.

I certainly am not. But my mother isn't going to search for a perfect sitter, and my father isn't about to get involved. Karen and Brian go next door in their cage, into the garage. It's summer. The garage should have been perfect, but it wasn't. And it wasn't my choice to make.

"They died," Sarah tells me.

She's so matter-of-fact. Karen and Brian had black eyes like the beads I would string on friendship bracelets. Brian was entirely black, Karen entirely white. The two created so much poop. My father cleaned the cage in shorts and an orange T-shirt, spraying the bottom with a hose.

"I've never seen so much fucking shit." He'd curse and stomp and remind me that these guinea pigs were mine and I had promised to clean the cage. But then he'd do it again the next week.

I would hold Karen and Brian every morning, petting their soft fur. My father is allergic to cats, and no one wants a dog, so Karen and Brian are the compromise. They live in the basement in a glass cage, and I kiss them and love them and hold them when I'm scared.

The first time my father leaves me alone in the house, I am six. He is just walking to the corner to buy a newspaper, a five-minute trip. I tell him I am fine, a big girl, practically a grown-up. But when he comes home I am behind the couch, crying. Karen is beside me.

"*Shh*," I whisper into her fur. "Don't be scared. Daddy will be home soon."

Karen and Brian had made babies by the dozen. This was a big surprise to us; we'd been told they were two females, which was bad information. We bred them again and again. Tiny litters of guinea pigs would appear and then disappear. My dad worked out a deal with the pet store: one guinea pig baby per bag of food. So it went for two years. We had inadvertently become breeders, bringers of guinea pig life.

And now these deaths. "Dead?" I ask my mother. Certainly I'd heard wrong. A neighbor's dog had found them in the garage. He'd bitten off their heads and left them on the back porch of our other neighbor's home—like offerings. But that's not what my parents tell me.

"Heart attacks."

I nod, but I am not sure what that means. I imagine their tiny hearts leaping out of the cage of their breastbones and charging through the rest of their bodies, murdering their spleen and their lungs—all that made Karen and Brian strong.

I don't cry. "Where are they?" I ask.

Mom is busy unpacking, but she pauses and takes my hand. "They already buried them."

The next day Sarah and I hold a ceremony. Her family buried them in the space between our properties in a patch of dirt where we usually play, plant flags, and make forts. It's home base for tag. Now it's my guinea pigs' eternal resting place.

"Should we say a prayer?" Sarah asks.

I don't know any prayers. She does, though, so she says a few Hail Marys. I don't know what it means, but the ritual seems to make sense.

We dig them up with little shovels, the plastic ones that come with beach buckets and rakes. We dig for a while before we hit the shoe box and pull it out. Karen and Brian are still intact, their fur still bright and obvious. The box is teeming with life: bugs, ants, and maggots. We put the box back quickly. There must have been a smell, the stench of death. Years later, when a mouse dies in the apartment I share with my husband, I will vomit into the toilet. Not because of the mouse that died in my bedside table, but because the smell will recall my friends, Karen and Brian.

My mother tells me that she believes all living beings are energy and that Karen and Brian have just been returned to the *prana*, the universal energy that surrounds us all. I like this idea. I imagine them as beams of light that I can move and manipulate with my hands.

"It flows in and out of all of us," Mom says.

The old man across the street who always tells us not to use his lawn. Prana. The wild boys down the street who jump and punch the air and break-dance to loud music played on old boom boxes. That's prana, too. Prana is neutral and it's in every interaction.

"It's all prana. Everything," she tells me.

But I still want to know and understand. We dig Karen and Brian up every day for the rest of the summer. We watch their fur start to mat. The bugs start to disappear. Their bones start to appear. I am horrified, but can't stop. It's fascinating and repulsive and alluring all at once. We dig and dig and dig for months, until one day we just forget, and we move on.

Ouija Board Fight

My eighth birthday is a loud affair, held at the local Chuck E. Cheese. That's where I receive a Ouija board wrapped in colorful balloon wrapping paper. But it's the pair of earrings a friend and I stole a month ago while our mothers were shopping that capture my attention. We slipped them into my friend's purse while the storekeepers weren't paying attention, but we quickly realize that my mother will notice if I am suddenly wearing earrings she has never seen. So we devise a plan.

I spend the next few weeks, leading up to my party, telling my mother how much I want a certain pair of teddy bear earrings from Claire's Boutique. I tell her that my friend is going to get them for me. I wrap them in newspaper, as though they were a gift, and now I present them to myself at the party. My big mistake was that I had written the card!

This immediately ends my life of crime. I crack under pressure and confess the entire dirty plot. My mother marches me to Claire's, where I return the earrings, red-faced and crying.

The Ouija board therefore slips in under the radar. In all the chaos of the birthday party blunder, I'd forgotten about the board. A couple of weeks later, Sarah is at my house and we get bored. It's pouring rain, the kind that sounds like a million nails hitting the roof. We keep looking out the window, but the day is promising to get gloomier, and it's only ten o'clock in the morning.

"I have a new game," I tell her.

"What kind?"

The thing about being an only child is that you never have anyone to play board games with. Sarah has her older brother and her slightly younger sister to play Monopoly, Life, and Sorry with at all hours of the day (as I assume they do). Whenever I have an opportunity to play, I do it with enthusiasm. I play with gusto and to win. I want to keep playing until someone's playing hand falls off. Sarah knows this. She's not so into it.

"It's called a woo-i-gee," I say, giving my best approximation of the correct pronunciation. The board is still wrapped in plastic, so I dig my nails in to pull it off. We read the directions, and Sarah remembers that her mother has told her not to play with Ouija boards, that they are bad and even dangerous.

Sarah and her family are Catholic. Her father is the principal of a local Catholic high school, and her mother had once entered a convent. Sarah is wearing a plaid jumper. It's a bit frayed around the bottom because she and her sister always stay in their uniforms after school. I envy these uniforms and that Sarah and her sister have a plan on how to dress every morning in the same outfit, with their Peter Pan collared shirts and knee socks. No jewelry is allowed. Sarah is almost always in sneakers, but her sister wears brown clogs, which are perfect. Having a sister just one year apart in age and never fighting over clothing or who gets to wear what jewelry sounds great. I am jealous.

Sometimes we joke that Sarah should have had my parents. She likes to break rules. She likes to go against what she learns in Catholic school and push the boundaries her parents set. So the Ouija board is right up her alley.

We pull the board out. We are eager to ask it all kinds of questions: What will I be when I grow up? Will I be rich? How many kids will I have? We set the board between us and place our fingertips on the planchette. Nothing happens.

"Will I ever have a sister or a brother?" I ask.

Nothing. No movement.

"I think we need to close our eyes and think hard," I tell Sarah. Still nothing.

"This is broken," Sarah says, and I can tell I'm losing her interest, so I give it a little push, just a small nudge. It makes a big leap. Sarah looks at me, her eyes wide.

"Did you do that?"

I shake my head. I am not sure. I think I gave it a nudge, but it wasn't a hard shove. Yet the planchette moved like it had been shoved. I'm creeped out, but I keep going.

"Will I have a sister or a brother?" I ask loudly, wondering if the spirit is hard of hearing. The planchette starts to glide toward No and then makes a sudden curve toward Yes.

We learn that the spirit we are talking to is a young boy who died in my house fifty years ago. I'm not surprised at all because I always suspected there was a spirit or a ghost in the house. This is vindication for all the times I sought it out, knocking on walls and listening for return knocks.

I want to believe the house is haunted because then I'd be less alone. It would be like having a sister or a brother, only they would be in ghost form. But beggars can't be choosers. My ghost brother's name is Charlie, or so he says.

"Do you know if a little boy named Charlie ever lived in this house?" I ask my mom later. She's making a tuna noodle casserole (this is before she goes macrobiotic), and the burner is on too high.

"Shit," she yells, and I hear the mushroom soup sizzling. She bangs her elbow as she tries to get the pan off the burner before the soup (which will be added to the casserole) is ruined. I don't care. I'm too excited. So what if the casserole is a little scorched?

"Do you know what a woo-i-gee board is?"

"Yeah, sure," she says, holding her injured elbow. "It's a spirit board. It's pronounced wee-gee."

"Okay. Ouija board." I tell her that I got one for my birthday, but she's not listening and I can tell, so I don't mention Charlie.

Two days later my mom and dad pull me into their bedroom while Sarah is playing in the living room with my favorite Barbie dolls. "We are going to have a baby," they tell me, their arms wrapped tight around each other. I am thrilled. I am crying, dancing, and screaming.

"Don't tell anyone," my parents call after me, but I am flying out the door toward Sarah.

"She's pregnant! My mom is pregnant! She's going to have a baby!"

Sarah is jumping up and down, and we are both crying and hugging. We run out the door into the neighborhood, screaming the news to anyone who will listen, like two pint-sized Paul Reveres—only instead of the Redcoats coming, it's a new baby. Within half an hour we have told the entire neighborhood, and my parents are too amused to be angry.

It's only as I am going to bed that night that I realize Charlie was right.

A few weeks later, my mother's belly seems to have grown overnight, but she's not due till January, and five months is an eternity for an eight-year-old.

Sarah and I have been talking to Charlie daily. My mother has been spending more and more time with her meditation and yoga group. Tonight the group's get-together is at our house. My father is out of town, and my mother is rushing around pulling together a snack. Sarah and I are eyeing the cookies.

"Don't touch those," my mother warns. Our kitchen is small and not fancy, but right in the center it has a built-in open-shelf system. Usually it's a jumbled mess, but today my mother has it organized with a few of her brass Hindu deities, a Buddha statue, and some beads.

"Just go upstairs," she tells me, making a shooing motion with her hand.

Sarah and I take off and pull out the Ouija board.

"Is my sister ever going to stop being annoying?" Sarah asks. Charlie says no.

"Is the baby going to be a boy or a girl?" Charlie says he doesn't know.

"Is it going to be sunny tomorrow?" Yes.

We go on like this, asking silly questions that mean a lot to two eight-year-olds but almost surely mean nothing to anyone else.

We get bored and wander back downstairs. By now my mother's group is mingling. Her friend Jackie gives me a big hug. I've always loved Jackie. She's someone people describe as having soul. She's very tall, with a soft body that makes her warm and fun to hug, and her smile is always on high wattage. I'm fascinated by her chipped front tooth, an imperfection that makes her even more appealing.

She asks me about school. I go to a small Montessori school where almost all the classes are self-directed, which means I do a lot of reading and building with blocks and learning Spanish, but almost no math. I explain this to Jackie, who is laughing.

"Sasha is so precocious," she says to my mother.

I smile. We hear that a lot.

The talk turns to impending babies. Jackie is pregnant, too, but she is due soon and invites me to feel the baby moving inside her belly. It reminds me of the footage I've seen of the Loch Ness monster, its back skimming the surface, a head or a tail poking out, belying the many feet of the monster beneath the surface. I tell my mother this, and both she and Jackie laugh and laugh.

"Maybe I will ask the Ouija if your baby is a boy or a girl, too," I say, laughing with them. I *am* precocious. I am also cute. I can predict the future with my magic Ouija board.

Jackie isn't laughing any more. Like my mother, she comes from a strict Catholic upbringing: baptism, first communion, confirmation, and years of Catholic education and church on Sunday have shaped the women they've become. Although both of them have left rosaries for mala beads and church incense burners for sage, they are products of their upbringing, and the similarities can't be denied.

"You have a Ouija board?" Jackie says, her eyes on my mother.

Something passes between them that I am too young to understand, but the meditation is starting and Sarah is leaving, so I decide to go home with her. My mother nods her approval as she sits down in the circle. Sarah and I walk to her house, laughing and singing the whole 200 feet it takes to get to her front door.

When I get home a couple of hours later, I can't find my Ouija board. It's not where I left it, beside my bed. I find my mother cleaning up in the kitchen and demand to know where it is.

"I threw it out." She seems to think that this will be enough of an explanation, which it isn't. I demand to know why. I want it back right now.

"It's in the trash, Sasha. It's not coming out."

I cry. "Why?" I plead. "Why?"

I don't tell her about Charlie or the spirits in the walls. From the way she is looking at me, I am guessing it would hurt my case. She has her glasses on, and this means she is tired. Ready for bed. When she takes her contacts out, it's almost bedtime. Her eyes are red-rimmed, and I wonder if she's been crying.

"I didn't really register that you had one of those. We talked a lot about them tonight in my group. They are bad. Bad karma. Bad juju. Bad spiritual energy. Just bad."

This is unlike my mother. After all, my father has three boxes of pornographic magazines that sit in my bedroom closet. I know this because I have opened them again and again and been horrified by what's inside. A pictorial that particularly terrified me was in Hustler. A woman is spread open, her insides looking like raw meat, while a man sticks his head between her legs like some kind of horror-movie gynecologist. My parents discover that I have seen the magazines because I bring them to school and pass them out on the playground, as if I need to share the bad energy.

Neither of my parents reacted to that with much more than a sense of embarrassment and a few laughs at the dinner table. In other words, my parents were not big on judging civil liberties. So I was convinced that my right to own a Ouija board was being infringed on. I couldn't stand for it.

I screamed. I yelled. But my mother was unmoved. "I will not have that bad energy in this house," she said firmly. "Not with a new baby coming. Not with everything I am trying to do to rid this space, this body, this house, of bad energy. I mean, Reagan is bad enough."

Reagan was her trump card. When she brought him up, I was sunk because, no matter what, this greedy president stood in the way of all my parents loved and stood for. So if he liked Ouija boards, mine was a goner. But I had one card left to play.

"I thought you weren't Catholic anymore."

She's not playing. She laughs. "Old habits die hard," she says. "It's also not a Catholic thing. It's a spirit thing. I don't want that negative energy around."

I can't believe my mother would say something so mystifying. For all her liberal politics and pushing boundaries, the fact that she is making me get rid of the Ouija board feels out of character and wrong. I argue and plead, but her mind is made up.

"This isn't a negotiation."

I never see my Ouija board again. Later, when I am much older and in the middle of my first 200-hour yoga teacher training, my husband and I are waiting for a table in a restaurant bar in Province-town, Massachusetts. We come here every year for our wedding anniversary, and this year is special because it's our tenth—a whole decade. Just the week before, we learned something new: we are expecting our third baby. I am only about a month along, so it is still new and exciting. We sit in the lounge chairs, and Rob hands me a menu.

Suddenly I see a Ouija board and a number of board games to

our left. I laugh and pick up the board. "I haven't seen one of these since I was a kid."

We place it between us and begin asking questions. Of course, we want to know about the baby. I am sure the baby is a boy—mostly because I want a girl so badly, I am sure the universe won't grant me this wish. I have prepared myself for the boy I am sure I will have. I am ready and willing to accept another son. The board disagrees.

"Is this baby a girl?" we ask three times. Yes. Yes. Yes. The same answer, again and again.

"Who are you?"

"C-H-A-R-L-I-E."

Then I remember.

"I don't I want to do this anymore."

We put it away. Six weeks later, the results of my blood test come in. The baby is normal, healthy, and ready to gestate. Also, the baby is a girl. I nearly drop the phone when the nurse tells me.

Charlie called it.

My kids will never have a Ouija board. I burn sage in the house. I meditate on positive energy and try to see the divine light in all who cross my path. I get it now why my mother made me throw out that board. I wish I could tell her. I wish I could take back the things I said about Catholicism and tell her that I know all things are connected and that energy is real and that any time we open ourselves to bad energy, we invite it to stay.

No more Charlie.

Tarot Card Reading

My mother is on her bed, surrounded by tarot cards. I look at the photos and cringe. Too many boobs. Why do all the women have to be naked? My mother is focused. She moves them around. She furrows her brow. I touch the deck as she asks. I choose the card.

It's Death. I start to cry.

"It doesn't mean what you think it means," she says. "It's something else. A symbolic death."

But I'm ten, and death is death. The card is frightening.

"I'm going to die. Great cards, Mom. Awesome."

"It doesn't work that way."

I'm on a roll. What kind of mother tells her daughter she's going to die? Does she know I probably won't sleep tonight? That will be her fault.

She tells me it's all interpretation, like anything else. One person loves a certain show on television because it appeals to him or her. Someone else hates it for the same reason. This death card, with the snake and the trees and the leaves and the skeleton, doesn't have to mean imminent death or disease. It could mean a transformational shift.

I look down at my concave chest. Maybe it means something will grow. But when I look at the card with the dead leaves and barren trees, I don't know. I just don't know.

Auras in Death and Dying

My favorite class in high school is on death. We are one of the few high schools in the state to offer thanatology, the study of death and dying. Mrs. Vaughn is no taller than five feet, she wears her hair cropped short and tight, and she moves around the room as if she's plugged into a wall socket. There are rumors she is gay, but no one cares, because she is one of the most beloved teachers in the school. We get deep into thanatology.

She started teaching the class ten years ago as part of a grieving process for her sister, who had been murdered in a home invasion four years earlier. We talk about grief and the process of grief. We talk about different support groups, like the one she joined after her sister died: Parents of Murdered Children.

"It saved our lives," she tells the class, as tears roll down our cheeks and we line up to hug her, one by one, after class.

Like I said, deep.

I love everything about Mrs. Vaughn. I love her bizarre and hilarious stories about her eccentric family. I love her stories about working as a correctional officer in a jail. She was tiny, but she was tough. I can't imagine anyone being able to hurt Mrs. Vaughn. But most of all, I love her belief in things we can't see.

"I don't know what I believe about spirits and ghosts," she says, "but I don't think life ends after we die. I think we become energy." She talks about energy all the time. She has it in abundance, but she means a different kind of energy, the kind that runs from human to human, that powers us all and connects us. She tells a class full of conservative Christians that we are all made of light energy. She tells us this every day.

Today she's explaining different kinds of healing crystals and what they can do for the soul. Purple amethyst is for relaxing. Black tourmaline is to protect your energy. She goes through each stone, telling us what it means and how it affects our energy and our sense of self. It's stuff I have heard a million times, but hearing it from my favorite teacher in my favorite class changes things. Maybe it's true, after all.

None of this is necessarily relevant to the study of death. But metaphysics and energy and working with the light are all part of the same family of yoga, and as I listen I am sure there is a reason this keeps coming up. At home, on my dresser, I have an amethyst, a bit of black tourmaline, and a peridot (for abundance) that my mother gave me last summer in a small, decorative box.

"These rocks are charged and ready to bring everything you need into your life," she tells me. I roll my eyes, but as I hold the rocks in my hand I can swear I feel them vibrating. They have stayed on my dresser ever since—just in case.

Matt Lindquist isn't buying any of this energy talk. I hear a shuffle in the back of class and turn to face him as he slams his giant hands down on his small wooden desk. The noise is startling, and half the class jumps. Lindquist is a football player. Every Friday he wears his jersey like everyone else in the school is supposed to. We are school spirit personified, wearing green and white as if it's our religion. For some of us, like Matt, it nearly is. If I understood or cared about football, I would understand why he is so revered, why he is on prom court and homecoming court, why he is voted prom king each year, and why, by the end of senior year, he has impregnated one of the blondest cheerleaders. By the age of nineteen they are the parents of a little girl and divorced.

But now he's frustrated and "just asking a question. Is this, like, devil stuff?"

Mrs. Vaughn laughs. "What do you mean. Matty?"

"Like, I don't know what other people think. But my pastor said all this stuff is bad. Like evil."

"Yes, but what 'stuff' do you mean?"

"Like talk of crystals and energy and witch stuff." Matt is looking around the room for support, and a few girls nod enthusiastically.

Chrissy Vawner, a sophomore cheerleader with an obvious crush on Matt, looks at him and smiles before raising her hand. "I agree, Mrs. Vaughn. All this feels like hell talk. Like we are going to go to hell if we believe it. Like it is against Christ."

I cringe. *Hell.* That word again. I am familiar with this line of thinking. I have been hearing it ever since I came to this school, and even before. When I was seven, my parents hired a new babysitter. Tracy was seventeen and lived down the street. She was fond of the color red. She always wore a red sweater or red pants and a giant red ribbon in her hair. She smelled like perfume and she wore thick, black eyeliner, just like Madonna. Tracy also weighed at least 250 pounds. This only made her seem more commanding and exciting, as though she were bigger than any of us could imagine. She took up space. She was someone to know. When I saw her and her fifteen-year-old sister, I longed to talk to them. I wanted to know all about what it was like to be in high school and to date boys—to be "big."

When Tracy came to babysit, I prepared. I carefully put out the ingredients to bake brownies. I put Monopoly and Life and Sorry in the living room. I wrote a list of questions I wanted to ask: Do you still like to roller skate now that you are grown up? Have you ever kissed someone? Do you have one best friend like me, or do you spread the love?

Tracy had another plan. As soon as she showed up, she started talking Jesus.

"Do you know our Lord and Savior?"

I was seven. "No. Do you want to play Monopoly?"

"I am worried for your soul," she told me. She showed me pamphlets, which I could barely read, but from what I understood, my father's Judaism and my mother's devotion to yoga pretty much guaranteed me a one-way ticket to a fiery underground.

"I don't mean to be mean or to scare you," she said, "but you are definitely going to hell if I don't help."

I didn't argue. I couldn't. She was a big girl who knew what she was talking about, and if I was going to hell, what about my parents? They started it. I could still be saved, but they couldn't. When my parents came home that night, I was wide awake and terrified. I didn't tell them why. I told them I was scared of monsters and they checked my closet. "No monsters," they assured me.

I insisted. I pleaded. I sobbed. They were patient at first. My father read me a story. My mother tickled my back. Then patience became anger. "Go to bed," my mother commanded, as she slammed the door behind her.

I lay in the dark, my eyes wide open, my heart pounding, my fingers shaking so much I couldn't keep the covers around me. I was going to hell. My mom was going to hell.

"Mommy! Mommy! Mommy!" But she'd had enough, so she ignored me.

I got out of bed to go to my parents' room, but the door was locked. I slid my hand in the space between the bottom of the door and the top of the carpet. My little hand fit perfectly. I knew if I could just reach my fingertips into their room, I would be close enough to keep them safe. They would also be close enough to keep me safe. If we were going to hell, we'd go together.

After that night, they never asked Tracy to babysit again. I never let my parents turn the light out again, either. It would be almost ten years before I would be able to sleep without a night-light or some reminder that the devil wasn't going to come up from hell and pull me down below where I would burn for eternity—just for the sin of having been born to two heathens.

Mrs. Vaughn is not fazed by Matt and Chrissy's objections, and her demeanor brings me back to the present.

"Why do you think that, Chrissy?"

I love Mrs. Vaughn.

"I mean, it's just against everything we learn in church."

"Is it?" Mrs. Vaughn always knows what to say. She grabs the rolled-up screen from the ceiling and pulls it down with a whooshing noise. Tapas. This is Sanskrit for "to heat," which Mrs. Vaughn is doing now by harnessing her fire energy and letting it fly.

This is what I do every time I run through my neighborhood, feet flying and hands pumping. Tapas. Tapas. Tapas. I am all in. She starts doing some jumping jacks and tells us all to get up and move because "this is going to blow your minds."

I am ready. I want my mind blown. I get up and dance and shake and laugh as Mrs. Vaughn punches the air and kicks her legs. "Okay, guys. Here it is. You think we are all made in God's image, right?"

She climbs up on a desk and holds up her arms. "See, now I am preaching."

Chrissy laughs nervously. Matt frowns and shifts in his chair.

"These ideas are not incompatible." She hops down and stands in front of the white screen, arms outstretched. She's in a five-pointed-star yoga pose: legs straight, heart up to the sky, gaze lifted. "Read me, guys."

Mark Manson raises his hand. He never talks in class, but he always listens even as he doodles pictures of guitars and cars in his notebook. I've never seen him do anything other than draw and listen. Mrs. Vaughn nods at him, and he speaks.

"Read you? What do you mean?"

The whole room laughs. I know what she means because my mother has taught me all about auras and the light that shines from within us all and the way we can use the energy that radiates from others to improve our relationships. "As long as you can read auras," my mother explained, "you can understand moods and how to treat people."

I am guessing that I am the only one in class whose mother has a copy of *Hands of Light*, a classic book that describes all the kinds of energy we feed on and wade through without ever realizing it—like static, which you notice only when it pins two socks together in the dryer. It radiates from us all.

"She means auras," I say, and everyone looks at me.

Chrissy looks me up and down. I am a freshman, and my hair is ribbonless and drab. She's perky and rosy-cheeked, and the ribbon in her hair is green and big. But I still know more about this than she does.

"They are the energy fields all around us," I explain.

Mrs. Vaughn holds her finger to her nose and uses the other to point in my direction.

"Sara gets a cookie. She's right. We all have them, whether we choose to believe it or not. And they are not incompatible with the teachings of Christianity. You can believe in energy and still believe in heaven and hell, although I do not."

The room goes quiet. Something unlocks inside me. I think of Tracy and my friend, Jamie, who tried to get me to join her at youth group. "If I can get you baptized," she told me, "I'll feel that I set my soul right for life. No offense, but you are definitely going to hell if you don't get right with Jesus."

I've heard this again and again. In seventh grade my biology teacher refused to teach us evolution without adding a unit on creationism. My parents complained, and I became the face of heathens everywhere. So to hear a teacher say she rejects a basic Christian belief, to hear a teacher offer another point of view beyond the Bible Belt religious crusade I've known my whole life, is something else.

"No offense, but if you don't believe in Jesus, I can't sit here," Matt says. He stands up from his desk, all six-foot-four of him, his body making everything around him look small, especially Mrs. Vaughn. But she is a force.

"Sit down, Matty. You might learn something."

The room is tense. A pulse moves through us all. We all know this could go either way. I wonder if Matt will storm out of the classroom. That would be a story. But he doesn't. He sits back down.

Once she has control of the room again, Mrs. Vaughn asks us to close our eyes. I do. I assume everyone else does, too. "Clear your minds. Focus on the third eye, the space between the eyebrows."

I am thinking that this is my jam. I know all about this, and I want to kiss and hug her and do a dance because finally someone in this high school—in the middle of a cornfield full of farmers and preachers' kids—is actually showing up. I am focusing. I am seeing the purple light in a way I never have. I imagine it there, burning bright and igniting the Ajna (third-eye) chakra. I can feel it for the first time, and not because my mother told me to, but because Mrs. Vaughn did. I am breathing. I am with the light.

"Open your eyes."

I see light bursting from her body in all directions. The white screen background highlights it all, and I see blue emanating from her shoulders, orange from her head, and all around her pelvis there is a red glow like nothing I have ever seen. I feel it in my belly, like something moving inside me, like a million fireflies lighting up. I feel warm and soft, as though something inside me has expanded and I can't make it go back.

"What do you see?" she asks.

I want to raise my hand. I want to hug everyone. I am so full of love, and I see the spirit, the one my mom sees.

Matty raises his hand. "I don't see nothin.'"

"Me, either," Chrissy says.

Everyone chimes in except Mark. I feel like crying. I am stunned. How can I be the only one? I stay silent because I am a weirdo, which I already knew, but I *really* know it now. When I look at Mark, he isn't drawing. His eyes are soft and he is looking right at Mrs. Vaughn, as I did. He sees it, too. I can just tell. I suddenly know I am not the only one. It's just that the others will not let themselves see the truth.

The Aura Book and Show-and-Tell

It takes me a full day to tell my mother about the aura class, mostly because I don't think she likes Mrs. Vaughn. She told me the week before that she is too informal, too much like one of the kids. "She's just not professional," my mom said. But I don't think it's only that. I've had many teachers who aren't professional and who want to be friends with the kids. I've had teachers who go off the curriculum and have us watch *The Man in the Iron Mask* as some kind of lesson in world history. So I can't imagine why Mrs. Vaughn gets under my mother's skin so much.

"I can't explain it," she snapped, so I let the subject drop.

This is why I wait to tell her about the aura class. I want her to know what I saw, and I want to know if she thinks it's significant. But it's bad timing. My father is away, and my mother is in a bad mood all the time. Tonight is trash night, and we live on a big hill. She asks me for help carrying the bags of garbage to the curb, but I am watching a show, and I ask if she can wait.

"I told you to help me now," she says, her eyes narrowed.

"And I told you I am watching *Roseanne* right now. I will help later."

She grabs my arm so hard, I suck in air. "Get up," she says. "Get up now."

"After the show." I shake her hand off me and rub my arm. "Really good parenting, Mother."

She glares. I can see how angry she is, but I also know her well enough to know she's going to back down. Once she gets physical, she has lost control. I have won. She storms out and takes the garbage out by herself. When she comes back, I call out to her, "I told you I would have helped you after the show."

She says nothing, but I hear her behind me in the kitchen, a knife scraping across the cutting board as she slices, dices, and chops.

"What's for dinner?" I ask.

"Get up and find out."

I don't. Later, when she puts a baked potato, steamed broccoli, and a chunk of a chewy protein substance in front of me, I balk, feeling disgusted. "What is this? And is there butter for the potato? Sour cream?"

"It's tempeh," she says. I can tell I am on thin ice, but she's trying to be calm. "We are out of butter and sour cream," she informs me.

My sister picks up her fork and starts to eat, and my mother smiles at her. "Good girl, Mashi," she says, calling Mariel by her nickname. "You always love to try Mommy's new foods, don't you?"

My sister smiles up at her and then looks at me, as if she's daring me to say something. So of course I do. "This is gross and I am not eating it, and if Dad were home he'd make sure we have butter and sour cream. Who the hell eats a baked potato plain?"

"I don't fucking care what you eat or don't eat!" Mom yells, slamming her hands on the table. "This is dinner."

My fork leaps into the air and lands on the floor with a clang. My sister and I are stunned into silence. I lean over and pick up the fork. I stab my broccoli spears and bring them to my mouth, chewing with obvious anger. *Look what you made me do. Look how grossed out I am by this crap you call food.*

I push the tempeh around on my plate. I am really hungry. I know I have to try it, so I take a bite. *Shit,* I think. *This is actually kind of good.* The marinade is spicy and delicious, and the tempeh is not nearly as bad as I expected. I take a few bites in silence. I can't tell her I like it, though. It's too late.

I watch my sister. She has yellow streaks of paint on her arm and spackle around her lips. I figure a kid who eats paint and spackle probably doesn't know that tempeh is gross and meat is better.

My mother is breathing deeply—in through the nose, out through the nose. I know the breath. She's angry, but she's using Ujjayi breath. In Sanskrit it means "victorious." She's the mom. She wins.

Later she is in her study while my sister, still covered in paint and sprawled out like a cat, is asleep on our bright red velvet living room couch. I love that couch. It was a gift from my grandparents when I was born, and now my sister is drooling on it. She needs to go upstairs and go to sleep. It's ten o'clock and the house is mostly dark, but I can hear my mother. It sounds as though she is crying. I peer inside. She's in the corner, perched on a thick, green-flowered chair, focused on her writing. She doesn't even notice I am there. She is definitely crying. I want to ask her what's wrong. I want to comfort her. But I am also angry.

I back away into the living room. Mariel has shifted and is sleeping on her other side, her little feet curled around a pillow, and she's quietly snoring. I pick her up. I put her in her bed and turn on her rainbow night-light. The yellow paint is still all over her arm, so I go to the bathroom, wet a pink washcloth, and come back to the room. It takes only a few wipes to get her clean, and she barely stirs. I know she should brush her teeth and put on pajamas, but she's fast asleep, so I figure one night will be okay. I turn out her light and make my way out of the room. She turns over and starts to snore again.

I am in my room, finishing some homework, when I hear my mother come up the stairs. I try to gauge from her footsteps whether she's still angry, if she wants me to come anywhere near her. I decide to take a chance.

I walk toward her door. This time it's shut all the way, so I knock. She doesn't answer. I knock again. This time she tells me to come in, and I do. She's in a long, white nightgown and is already under the covers, with a Dick Francis novel in hand.

"What do you want?"

"I wanted to tell you about class yesterday. Something cool happened."

"Sasha, I am exhausted. I am pissed. You really acted like an asshole tonight. Can you tell me tomorrow?"

I know she's right, and I know I did, but I think she acted like an asshole, too. Yet I know if I tell her this, I won't get anywhere, and I want more than anything right now to tell her what I learned and how I finally see some of what she's been telling me all these years. So I don't tell her that I think she's being a jerk. I just stand there, shifting my weight from foot to foot.

"I put Mariel to bed. She was asleep on the couch. I washed her face and stuff."

My mom nods. "Good. Thanks."

That's an in.

"I'm sorry," I say, because I am. "I don't know why I act like that."

"When I ask for your help, I need you to help me. It's hard doing this all alone."

I nod. I know. "I'll be better. Can I tell you my story now?"

Her body language changes. She softens as though she's been holding her breath all this time. "Okay. Tell me."

"So you know Mrs. Vaughn?"

Mom tilts her head and looks at me as if to say, *you know how I feel about her.* And I do.

"This is really cool. I promise."

"Okay, out with it. What is so cool?"

"I saw Mrs. Vaughn's aura."

Mom looks at me and raises her right eyebrow. It's a trick I inherited, and I know exactly what it means: Yeah, right, kid.

"It was blue, mostly. But it had some orange at the head."

She yawns and stifles a grin. "Okay?"

"I thought you'd be interested. Also, there was a whole bunch of red, right around her hips."

My mother looks directly at me. "Wait, really?"

I nod. Does this mean something?

She grabs my hand. "I have to show you something." She pulls me down the stairs, flipping light switches as we go. The tile is cold under my bare feet, and it must be close to midnight, but I am wide awake. She opens the door to her study and turns on the overhead light. Her journal is still out and open on her chair, and I make a mental note to look at it tomorrow and see what she said. But tonight she's pulling books down off the shelf. Finally she finds what she is looking for.

Hands of Light is a big book, and the front cover seems hokey. White hands are held slightly apart with a beam of white-light energy between them. My mother is flipping through the pages excitedly. At one point she stops at blue: thyroid energy, calm, peaceful. I see these words as she flips toward the back and holds the book out to me. "Is this what it looked like?"

The photo shows a celestial body of white light surrounded by different colors. There are layers of colors, each one on top of the one before it, making an almost rainbow-like effect. I only saw one bit of light coming off Mrs. Vaughn's body. I didn't see these layers. But I did see the red coming from her pelvic region. I explain this to my mom, and she nods.

"You wouldn't see it all right away. Not the first time. And not everyone can see any of it at all. You are lucky. But I knew it when you told me about the red. It's the sexual color. I believe you that you saw it. It's amazing." She grabs my hands and holds them. "You are an asshole sometimes, Sasha. But you have a light. You can see things. It's a gift."

I can see things.

Guilt Trips from My Own Daughter

I am heading out the door, but the guilt never stops. So many times I stand on the back deck, with the knob of the back door in my right hand, wondering if I should go back inside. Every time my little girl cries, I wonder if I am doing her a disservice.

The reality of being a yoga teacher is that it's a practice. The 200-hour training is intense. There are dozens of ways the time is divided. My mother took a longer version that was offered over three two-week periods. My first 300-hour training is a six-month comprehensive that includes a bonus certification in prenatal yoga. I spend every other weekend in the studio, along with every Wednesday and Friday night. A few months later I do another 200-hour intensive with the same schedule. During the second one, I also taught and practiced every day.

If my daughter thinks that I am always gone, it's because that feels true to her. I am gone every other night, either teaching or training. I practice so I can grow as a teacher. Sometimes that means leaving in the evening, but it often means waking at five o'clock to make it to my local studio's 5:45 AM class.

The dishes are piled up in the sink. The center island of our kitchen holds three school art projects, a mysterious set of keys that has been there since early fall, three bowls full of rotting fruit, and a package of wipes.

I could stay home and clean. The living room is piled with toys, the dining room is stacked with papers of unknown origin, and there is something sticky on the couch. I see all this as I head out the door. If I don't get in the car in the next three minutes, I will be late. I will miss the opening meditation to tonight's four-hour training.

"Maybe someday you'll understand," I tell my daughter, echoing another conversation from another time. I know she will, so I close the door behind me as I leave.

5. FLOWING

THIS IS THE CULMINATION OF ALL THE WORK.
THE DANCING, FLOWING VINYASA.
THE BALANCES, STRENGTH POSES,
HIP OPENERS, AND STRETCHES,
ALL THROUGH BREATH.

First Meeting with Gurudev

A few days after the aura excitement, it's time to see Gurudev. Janet's mother calls the night before to chat with my mother about it. I only hear my mother's end of the conversation, of course, but I recognize the way her tone changes. She is in full yoga teaching mode.

"There is some chanting in Sanskrit, yes. No, there is no bowing down or worshipping unless you want to. *Guru* means teacher, not god. There might be some movement, but no weird devil stuff."

My mom laughs as they get off the phone, so I know she's convinced her.

I am not surprised that Janet's mother has called. It's not the first time my parents have to talk her into letting Janet do something with us. A couple of summers ago we planned a trip to New York City to visit my uncles, and they thought it would be fun for me to bring a friend. Janet was the obvious choice, but her mother wasn't so sure about her staying with two gay men.

"It just seems weird," she told my mother.

My mother used her calm, cool tone then, too. "Them being gay has nothing to do with what wonderful people they are. It's a great opportunity for Janet. She will love to spend time with them."

Mom didn't say anything on the ride home from that visit, but I knew what she was thinking. I have often wondered why all my parents' friends live on the other side of town or in Manhattan or London. My parents don't sit on the sidelines at my tennis matches or go out for drinks with the other parents after my band concerts. My mother doesn't wear a bikini on the concrete walkways surrounding the Jewish Community Center pool, and she certainly doesn't flirt with the lifeguards and talk about how cute they are.

I think it's because she is at least a decade older than many of them. She had me when she was twenty-eight, much later than most of the other parents had had their kids. My parents don't enjoy drinking, football, or homecoming parades. "It's just shallow," my mom explains.

I don't get it. I want them to be like the others, sitting on the sidelines and giggling about the coaches and all the latest teacher gossip, discussing the finer points of tackling or whatever those football-loving parents discuss every Friday night as they shiver on the sidelines under three blankets and the bright lights of the stadium.

My parents march on Washington for abortion rights. They stuff envelopes for Planned Parenthood.

In 1992, after the riots sparked by the police beating of Rodney King, Janet and I write a letter to the editor of the *Dayton Daily News* calling racism to task. We ask that the world listen to the voice of two fourteen-year-old girls, since it isn't listening to anyone else.

Janet's mother, however, asks the paper to remove her daughter's name. "I am not comfortable with her having her name attached to that," she says. "What if someone comes to our house to get her?"

I remember thinking that I do not belong here in this tract hous-ing subdivision with people who care more about making it to band practice in the afternoon than how institutional racism is destroying our culture. I am angry at the apathy and the ignorance. But I am also angry at my parents.

"Why can't you just be normal?" I ask again and again.

My letter is published in May 1992. It is the first piece I publish in a newspaper outside my school. One of the more popular boys, a big blond who had deflowered my close friend Jessica a few years before, challenges me to an open debate in front of the whole school.

"I'll show her what's right," he tells Jessica, who relays the message to me.

That debate never happens, but many others do. I am the only person in my entire speech class who is able to take the pro-choice side during our debate on abortion. On the other side is Jenny, a hulking girl with frosted blond hair and an unreasonable amount of facial hair, who was my friend in middle school but whose extreme Christian views have made me shy away from her in high school.

"My mother has breast cancer," I tell the class. "If she got pregnant again, she'd die. You really would oppose abortion for her?"

"You'd still have your father," Terri says, raising her man-size fists into the air and encouraging applause from the rest of the class, including the teacher.

This is my school, in my town. When Janet's mom is sure her daughter will go straight to hell if we take her to Gurudev's lecture on being more present and mindful in our daily lives, it shouldn't come as a surprise. Yet it does, every time.

I love Janet's mom. She's funny, loving, beautiful, and "one of the girls" in a way no other mother I know could possibly be. She knows all the kids at school. She coaches drill team and cheerleading and had become a teacher after receiving her bachelor's degree, her master's degree, and eventually her PhD. She is no slouch. That's why her adherence to the rules of propriety and her fears about religion and speaking out always surprise me. They never surprise my mom, though, which is why her measured response is annoying.

"Mom, did she really ask you if this is devil stuff?"

"She was concerned," my mom says. "Now she's not."

Later that night, as she is putting my sister to bed, I go into her room and retrieve her journal from its place by the bed.

Yoga and the devil. Sometimes I can't even begin to understand the way people think in this town.

I am vindicated. I know now that my mother sees it as I do, even if she doesn't say so. She sees that we are like oil in water in this town, a square peg in a round hole, a million clichés that all boil down to one big fact: We don't belong here. We never will.

When the day comes to visit Gurudev, I wear an outfit my mother bought for me at the ashram. It's a batik print, white on blue, with stretchy pants and a long flowing shirt. It will be years before Lululemon enters the scene, and my mother is even more strangely dressed, in head-to-toe white linen. We are in the ballroom of a big hotel in downtown Dayton, where the sterile walls and patterned carpet look out of place among the sheer amount of love and devotion among the hundreds of people dressed like my mother and ecstatically hugging one another.

My mother is smiling and laughing with her meditation group. She's pulling people into group hugs and touching their foreheads. At one point, she and a man I've never seen before put their foreheads together and hold like that for a minute or more, their eyes open and staring at the ground. He has a long gray ponytail. Even if I believed that men should have ponytails, especially over the age of fifty, his is entirely too long. It hangs nearly to his waist, and his hands, wrapped around my mother's hips, are long and spindly. They have sprouts of gray hair, both above and below the knuckles, and his shirt is unbuttoned enough to reveal the same horrible hair sprouting from his chest.

I am in hell, mortified. My face is burning red, and I keep looking at Janet. Is she horrified? Will she tell all the kids in the school what a freak my mother is?

"I'd like you to meet Gregor," Mom says, pulling me into an embrace with this strange old man. I practically elbow him to get away.

"I guess you aren't a hugger," Gregor says, and he's mostly right. I am not. Years from that moment, my fellow teachers at the studio where I spend most of my time will constantly pull me into hugs, trying to force me to become a hugger. I will awkwardly hug new people and wonder why yogis are all so into hugging each other.

It's not that I am not affectionate. I am—deeply. As an adult I want to hug my children and my husband every minute of every day. But I am also slightly claustrophobic, so the thought of being pulled in close to a person makes me squirm. I like to keep my personal distance from strangers, especially those I suspect may smell, and in Gregor's case that is a distinct possibility.

My mother laughs. Gregor tells me that she is the most beautiful woman he's ever seen. I suppress the urge to vomit.

"You know she's married, right?"

He laughs. "I just mean her soul," he says. "Her soul is beautiful. You are lucky she is your mom."

I don't feel lucky.

In the center of the room is a platform surrounded by orange, red, and yellow flowers, and just to the right of it is a giant black-and-white photo, draped with sandalwood beads and crystals. I recognize the man in the picture from a similar picture on my mother's altar. He is long and lean, and his head is completely bald, but his eyes are friendlier than Gurudev's. There is a light in them, and even though he is not smiling in the photo, I get the sense that soon after the photo was taken he burst into laughter, as if he took his practice and teachings seriously but didn't take life so seriously.

His name is Swami Kripalvanandji, and he is the one who taught Amrit Desai (Gurudev) all that he knows. Desai brought yoga to the West and founded Kripalu and an ashram in Pennsylvania; when he did so, he brought the teachings of this master, who is also called Bapuji.

I learn that this is how yoga is passed down—not by skinny white blond women in Lululemon at Whole Foods, but by one yoga master to another. Bapuji learned from his teacher, too. They practiced night and day, and eventually, when the teacher believed that the student was ready, the student was allowed to become a teacher. There was no 200-hour training. A teacher is more than a person who stands at the front of the class and leads an hour-long Asana practice.

I understand this as I walk into the room. Later, when I become a teacher, I will understand this even more. The opening chant in any ashtanga yoga practice is as follows:

Vande Gurunam Caranaravinde Sandarsita Swatma Sukhava
Bodhe Nih Sreyase Jangalikayamane Samsara Halahala Mohasantyai
Abahu Purusakaram Sankhacakrasi Dharinam Sahasra Sirasam Sve-
tam Pranamami Patanjalim
  Om.

I bow to the lotus feet of the Gurus,
The awakening happiness of one's own Self revealed, Beyond better, acting like the jungle physician, Pacifying delusion, the poison of Samsara.
Taking the form of a man to the shoulders,
Holding a conch, a discus, and a sword,
One thousand heads, white, to Patanjali, I salute.

Somewhere along the way this relationship between teacher and student will be lost, but it's still the early days of yoga in the West, and my mother is practically ecstatic with joy at the prospect of seeing her guru.

All this reverence has a dark side. For many male gurus—including, eventually, Amrit Desai, my mother's guru—the power goes to their heads. Eventually he will be rocked by sex scandals. But right now we know none of this. He is my mother's teacher, and she is in awe as he takes his place among the flowers and the beads.

Gurudev's voice is hypnotic. As we chant together, I watch as some disciples approach and kiss his feet. I look at my mother, mouth agape in horror. She smiles back at me. "Do you do that?" I mouth, and point in the direction of the crazy foot kissers. She shakes her head, but the way she looks at him, I am not sure I believe her.

Gregor is in the line to touch Gurudev, as are several others. I notice they are all dressed in linen, like my mother. The colors are light, mostly whites and beiges and light browns, such a contrast to the brightness of the flowers and Gurudev's orange garment.

I begin giggling uncontrollably. Janet looks at me, her eyes wide. She places a finger over her mouth. "*Shh.*"

My friend Angel is there with her parents, and she seems to be more into it. She's not laughing. Her long brown hair is tied up in a high bun, and I can see her silver cross earrings. Those are the key thing about her. Her parents are weirdos like mine, but they aren't all in. They still attend church. They are still "normal." Her parents are holding hands and look content and peaceful, but they are not in adoration or in ecstasy.

My mom is. It's so embarrassing. I can't stop laughing.

Janet pokes me hard in the ribs. "Shut up. You are embarrassing."

My mother isn't looking at me at all. I finally get the laughter under control and start listening.

Gurudev is talking about the moment and how we can be more present. He is also talking about our thoughts and how they are *prana*, pure energy. When we think negative things about others, we are actually thinking those same things about ourselves, and the thoughts convert to negativity in our bodies.

I think of the things I have been thinking about my mom, Janet, my changing body, and my social life. I judge and judge and judge. Have I been judging myself? Is my fear of losing people making me hang on too tight? Has it become the thing that pushes them away?

I am crying. I can't stop. Fat tears are running down my cheeks, and my shoulders are shaking. I am so embarrassed. My mother reaches for my hand. Her hand is soft and cool, like when I was small and had a fever and she would run her hand across my forehead and I'd instantly feel more secure. It has the same effect here and now. My breath evens out. I smile, but I am laser-focused on Gurudev.

He speaks of the things we covet and how they hurt us in the long run. He speaks of the breath and how our continued focus on it allows for peace, even if we only find it in the space between the breaths.

Every sentence leads to new bursts of thought in my head. I want him to slow down so I can savor each one. I want to be alone in a room with him and have him explain everything to me.

Why do I fight happiness?

Why am I so consumed by the right clothing, the right car, and the right house? I've never had this experience in a church or a synagogue. This man's words are setting off a series of small explosions inside my head—the good kind, the type that create deeper awareness and sense of self.

I am hooked.

An hour has gone by, and I have barely noticed. People lock arms. I reach for Janet, but she's blowing bubbles with her gum and staring at the lines on her hand. She's bored. I know that look. I nudge her, and we lift our arms.

"Jai Gurudev! Jai Gurudev! Jai Gurudev!" English translation: Victory to the guru. And it is.

Because we say it together, and I realize I mean it. I have the urge to hug him, or at least to be close to him. This knowledge enters me, spreads like melted butter on toast, and sinks through my skin, warming me from the crown of my head to the tips of my toes. Something is happening.

My mother grabs my hands and kisses me. "See? Do you see now?"

I do. I see. I watch as people approach him. They bow and kiss his feet. I realize I want to kiss his feet, too. Jai Gurudev, indeed. As I approach the line, I gaze down. His feet are poking out from underneath his orange robe. I can see his toenails. They are long and yellowed.

Janet pokes my back. "They're kissing his feet?" she whispers. "This is super weird."

The spell is broken. Gross. I turn back toward my mom. "Can we get ice cream on the way home?" I ask.

Coming Back to Yoga

In 1995 I come back to yoga by accident. I had dabbled in college, sometimes walking into a yoga class when my running or elliptical routine became repetitive. Mostly, though, yoga felt like something long ago and far away: a breathing practice and a mindfulness I was trying to avoid. So instead I ran. I filled tape after tape with mixes of powerful music. *Eye of the Tiger. Kiss. Thriller.* I blasted it hard in my ears so that the only thing I felt was the pounding of my legs on the pavement and my heart in my chest. Thud. Thud. Thud. With every step, I was closer to something—some magic, some truth.

I ran my first 5K race at twenty-five. I was newly married and wanted to find a way to improve my running. It was a local race in Somerville, Massachusetts, and although I had been running for years, the only competitions I'd entered were the ones that happened inevitably to all marginally competitive runners who run next to someone faster. I would usurp them for a bit, then they would eclipse me. On and on we'd go, leapfrogging over strangers, improving our own game as we tried to beat one another.

I ran that 5K race in twenty-three minutes. If you aren't a runner, just know this: My time was "fastish"—not fast enough to win any medals or awards, but fast enough to make me want to run more, to get the dream all runners chase: the carrot, the personal record (PR).

Running also makes me sick. I spent the first twenty-four hours after that 5K race in the bathroom with "runner's trots." That's a euphemistic way of saying I had diarrhea and stomach cramping because I didn't know then that every runner has a magic formula: eating one particular food before a race, timed just perfectly to avoid the stomach problems that can come from going too hard, too fast, and too long.

Running does other things, too. I've strained my Achilles tendon, broken my ankle, strained my hamstring muscles, and tweaked my sacroiliac joint. I've dealt with inner knee pain and outer knee pain and had to tell pedicurists for years that I have nerve damage in my left big toe from running a marathon in shoes that were half a size too small. No one told me that your feet will swell over 26.2 miles and that you have to run in a slightly bigger shoe.

I've seen doctors, chiropractors, massage therapists, and acupuncturists. I've done cupping and stretching and physical therapy. Running is not for sissies. It's hard on the body, and some long runs on hot summer days have made me shed blood at the chafing points of my sports bra.

And the tears—always tears. It hurts so good.

The Achilles injury gets me into a yoga studio. Most injuries take a week or so to heal. That becomes a week of bicycling or rest and walking. Then I come back, better than ever. But I didn't come home one day with pain in the back of my leg from a fall or a stumble. I didn't roll over into a ditch on the side of the road or trip over a rock.

It was cumulative, a gradual wearing down, until one day the tendon stood up and said, *Hello. Pay attention now.*

Here. Now. It's a meditative breath. But I am not present in my body, not present to this pain. "When can I run again?" I ask my doctor, my massage therapist, and my acupuncturist. They all tell me to try yoga. I know it's not for me, and I want to say I have tried it—a million times. I can't calm the mind. I can't do it. I am bad at it.

We live close to a studio, though, and the pain is a seven on a scale of ten, so if yoga can get me back to running, I'll try it. I walk into Baron Baptiste's studio in Cambridge, Massachusetts. It's close enough to walk, and we only have one car.

I have never been in a yoga studio, despite the fact that I've been in a million places where yoga is practiced. In college we took it in a fitness room lined with Bosu balls, free weights, and TheraBands. Kripalu has grand halls, with windows on the sides, altars at the head of the room replete with statues of Shiva and Krishna, and stages where the teacher can direct the postures.

This is different. Here and now. Yoga is different in 2003. In the ten years since my mother died, yoga has exploded in the West. Studios have popped up all over the place, from small towns in Maine to big cities in California. Big name yogis release DVDs and show off muscular shoulders and spiritual enlightenment. They are beautiful, these yogis. Even though it will be another decade before Instagram comes on the scene, the cult of personality around the big-name yogis has already begun.

Of course, I know none of this when I walk into the Baptiste studio in Cambridge. I expect something austere, clean, and simple, like Kripalu. Baptiste is indeed austere. But from there it deviates. Pools of sweat can be seen on the soft carpet. The place smells like mildew and feet. The first class opens the door from the changing room to the studio, and steam follows them. They all look as though they've showered in their clothing, and their bodies look red and porous. The changing space is small and pure chaos. The old class is searching for bags, shoes, cell phones, and keys. The new class is finding places for all of our stuff. The heat from the studio wafts into the changing room, and we are all sweating before we've even started.

What the hell is this place?

I have no mat, so I rent one for an hour. It is wet and sticky with someone else's sweat, and I want to ask for Purell or some kind of sanitizing product, but I figure that's considered bad form. The mats are thin, thinner than any I have ever used. We line up outside the door, waiting for permission to enter. There are fifteen minutes between classes, so when the studio does open the doors, we file in and place our mats. The space is small, much smaller than it looks from the outside.

"Come on, file in." The teacher is a slight Scottish man with a red beard and muscled shoulders. He is sweaty in the extreme, as though he's just returned from a long swim in a lake. People know him. They hug him. They talk and laugh, and I wonder how they manage. The room is oppressive with the sweat of the seventy-five people who have just filed out and with the smell of the incense the teacher is burning in the corner. The smoke floats heavily in the air, forming a film that obscures the few lights. I do my best to avoid the pools of sweat the teacher is trying to sop up with a towel wrapped around his foot, but there are too many to get them all, especially as the room begins to fill.

"Use the tape. Use the tape." I ignore this directive and place my mat down, but a woman to my left immediately corrects me.

"Your mat has to go here," she says, pointing out small L-shaped pieces of tape that have been placed all over the hardwood floor. I think what she is telling me is impossible. There is less than an inch between mats. She assures me that is correct.

"First time?" she asks.

I nod, wondering what I am doing here.

"I am Patrick," the teacher shouts. "We need to make room."

I think we can't possibly fit another body into this space and that someone is going to have to practice on the sidewalk, but more and more people keep entering in their tiny shorts and sports bras, women with impossibly chiseled abs and men with what can only be described as Speedos. To my left, a man has taken the Supta Baddha Konasana (supine bound angle—soles of the feet together, knees splayed, back to the floor) pose, and I am seeing a lot more of his body than I want to.

The room gets hotter. I wonder how much worse it can get. Later I will learn. The temperature starts in the mid-nineties, but it morphs and changes according to the temperature outside and the number of bodies squeezed on top of one another.

We start to breathe.

Patrick is funny and inventive. He tells stories as we move. The concept of hot yoga is new to me, so I don't know I need a towel. Within minutes my mat is a mess of sweat. My hands slide forward, and the balls of my feet slide back.

"The pose need not be static," Patrick tells us, and I wonder if it ever could be. I am drenched, soaked so thoroughly that the skin on my hands has begun to shrivel. The poses seem impossible. We do six wheels; I can't even do one. Unlike the yoga I grew up with, Baptiste's version (an offshoot of power yoga) flows from one pose to the next. We move with the breath, but the poses are pure strength and balance: Eagle. Warrior. Plank. Plank. Plank.

I am only marginally familiar with the poses at this point in my life, so my elbows bend out to the sides in the Chaturanga pose, and I don't know how to modify it at all. Perhaps this is dangerous, and later, when I am a teacher, I will wonder this about Baptiste. There are no blocks, at least none that I see. There are no bolsters, no blankets, and no straps. People bend their knees to reach for their toes, and everyone looks different.

I hate every second of it. I hate the feeling of my soaking wet clothing. I hate the puckered wet foot in my face (hello, neighbor). I hate that I am pretty sure someone else's sweat dripped down into my butt crack during the Prasarita Padottanasana (Wide legged forward fold) pose. I hate that someone farts midway through the class and that the whole room smells of feet, farts, and salty gamy sweat.

I want to leave, but the door feels impossibly far away. The heat boils everything down to one tunnel of vision. My body is swimming in sweat, but my mind is becoming focused—focused on hate, yes, but that's hardly the point. It is singular and unscattered, unlike any other moment. No one ever said meditation had to be easy or that you had to like it. Patrick is funny. He takes the pressure off.

I watch my neighbor reach under her leg with her right arm and around the small of her back with her left arm to find a grasp. I can't even imagine being able to do this, but I am not envious. I am not frustrated or competitive. The heat makes all that impossible. But I *am* curious whether my body will be able to bend and mold and be shaped like clay if I keep coming back to the practice.

The class is ninety minutes, and by Savasana there is a pool of sweat under me.

"The prana (sweat) is all around. Be careful you don't release into it."

I can't imagine there is any other choice. We let go into puddles of sweaty saltwater and maybe some tears, too.

Prana that drips. Mats one inch apart. 100 degrees. This is not my mother's yoga.

When the door finally opens and we file out, the air outside is chilly and provides relief, even though I immediately shiver. The crisp air is refreshing. People smile in the crowded dressing room. Once you have dripped prana all over another person's skin, it is hard to see him or her as "other." It is hard not to smile.

I hated every second of my first class at Baptiste, but I knew I'd be back the next day and the day after that. Yoga had come back to me.

I tried to imagine my mother there, effortlessly gliding into a handstand or sweating so much that her hair hung in soaking strands down her back. But I couldn't. This was something else entirely, a deeply physical practice through which I could access the kind of spirituality I was comfortable with. After all, it's hard not to meet God when you think you might die of heatstroke.

There is no guru and no two-hour meditation to be done while seated upright and feeling uncomfortable. This is a practice I can feel.

The next day I feel sore and tired. My gluteal muscles are screaming, and my shoulders feel firm and locked. Somewhere in the space between the material world and the world of spirit and my mother is this practice. I know I am home.

Yoga as a Young Mom

"I miss you Mommy," Samara says, crawling on my back.

I think, *Missed me? But why? She's been home all day, sick.* We think she has the Coxsackie virus. She claims her feet and hands tingle, and I have obsessively checked her temperature all day: 99.4, 100.3, 101. Damn it. She will be home again tomorrow, and I will spend another day trying to plan class, read, and write while she watches *My Little Pony* on the flat screen.

"Mommy," she cries when I go the bathroom.

"Mommy," she cries when I go get the laundry.

"Mommy," she cries when I walk into the hall to let the dog into the backyard.

"Mommy," she cries when I sat on the chaise in the dining room for ten minutes.

I am sure she's not lying. I'm sure she misses me. How well I know that feeling—to miss. By definition it means to lack, to be without. I am without a mother. I miss her. But it can mean other things: literally, to fail to hit a ball—a swing and a miss; figuratively, to miss a promotion at work. It means to try and to fail. As a noun it means the failure to hit or make contact with something. What a word.

How does my baby mean it? Did she try to touch me, and she failed? Does she just miss me because I went into another room? The kind of longing I feel for my mother isn't adequately covered by *miss*. Not if my three-year-old can "miss" me in the next room. I long, I pine, I search for my mother in every face. I have seen her in a million celebrities: in Michelle Pfeiffer's high cheekbones and in Cher's long legs, in Madonna's sinewy arms and Carly Simon's huge smile. All these women have grown and changed, and in my mind, that's how she would have changed, too. She tried to age, to let her hair become gray before she was forty, to dump the contact lenses and wear glasses. But a forty-five-year-old has no idea what it is to be old, not really. A swing and a miss.

"Mommy go to yoga?" Samara asks, as I head out the door, mat in hand.

I left Baptiste years ago. Now I go to O2 Yoga, and it's the first studio where I feel truly at home. The practice isn't heated. It lives somewhere between the slow flow at Kripalu and the crazy pace of Baptiste. We do arm balances, twists, and binds. I buy a monthly pass and go every day. I write my name on my mat with a Sharpie so people know who I am.

Yoga is trendy now. Everyone I know does it. Blond women with tall lattes show up to class, towels in tow. They have the $100 mats and the pricey yoga tops with their built-in shelf bras and fabulous designs. "It's so relaxing," they say. And it is.

I still run every day. I've run two marathons and many half marathons, and I think yoga will never take over in my life. But I am wrong. My favorite teacher at O2 is a man named Elliott, who is bald

and looks a little like Christopher Meloni, who used to be in *Law &
Order: Special Victims Unit.*

We flow. Sun A's. Downward Dog to Utannasana (forward fold)
to Ardha Uttanasana (upright forward fold). We inhale to Urdhva
Hastasana (upward salute) and offer it back to the earth. We move
from high to low, from plank to Chaturanga, and now I am sure I was
doing it all wrong, sure my elbows were out to the sides and I was
placing undue pressure on my shoulders, but then it just feels good
in my body and mind and I don't care if I am doing it right or not.

Yoga had been painful for so long. I stopped, I started. I started, I
stopped. I didn't miss yoga for years. I didn't practice because I hardly
understood it enough to miss it. But this shift in the yoga world—the
movement away from hippie fringe counterculture baby boomers,
with their incense and Birkenstocks, to latte-drinking, upper-middle-
class moms in Boston—made it accessible again.

"My mom was a yoga teacher" got me street cred now. I didn't
have to hide it. It was no longer my secret shame, like "my mom was
in jail" or "my mom really liked Nickelback."

Yogis are still vegan or vegetarian. They still try to save the planet.
My studio is committed to recycling and lowering our carbon foot-
prints. Yogis prefer we bring our own water bottles and subscribe to
e-mail lists rather than ask for flyers. Saving the planet is trending now.

And the practice feels harder. Was it always this way? I never
saw my mother do anything more complicated than a headstand.
But now there are handstands and forearm stands. There are arm
balances—crow, Eight-Angle, Flying Pigeon. I never knew yoga was
so physical.

This is what keeps calling me back. But it's something else, too. I
am a writer and a mother. I spend most of my days with my children.

I wipe noses, cut grapes, push swings, and bounce toddler bums up and down on my legs. The children use me as their jungle gym, their home base, their napkin, and sometimes even their toilet. Sometimes my husband comes home and tries to hug me, and I just can't imagine another hand on my body.

So it's yoga: my mat, my prayer, my moving body.

The writing comes slowly. I got a master's degree in journalism five years ago and worked at newspapers and then at the news office at the Massachusetts Institute of Technology for several years. But none of it paid well, and once Samara was born I left the steady full-time gig for the realm of freelance writing: an essay here, a reported piece there; a profile, then two, then three.

But the frequent rejection was hard to take.

"No, sorry, this isn't us."

"Thanks, but we just ran this same story a few weeks ago. Did you check our archives?"

Those are the nice ones. There is also silence. I pitch a story idea to an editor, even one I know, and I don't hear back for days, weeks, months, or ever. Swings and misses, over and over.

"We hold our tension in our hips," the teacher reminds me, as I do a long pigeon pose. My right shin is parallel with the top of the mat, my arms are stretched out in front of me, and my forehead is to the mat. The stretch is all piriformis, the muscle that runs from the spine to the upper femur, which is a tight place for runners. From a physiology standpoint, there is a reason for my tight hips. I know this. But I know it's something else, too. Women hold our tension in our hips: our second chakra, Svadhisthana, the center of sensuality, pleasure, emotions, and desire.

Yoga moves all your energy though all the chakras and balances them. But these long holds that release specific chakras are particularly alarming. People panic in the pigeon pose. They cry. It's all part of the process, our teacher reminds us. The more I feel, the more I move and the more I release—in every breath, in every exhalation. I surrender, release, and melt.

I become a better parent. Yoga is just mine. It's also measurable. If I can't bind my hands around my thigh in an extended side angle one week but two months later I can, I see the measurable difference in my body. My shoulders are more open and my thighs are growing stronger—strong enough to support this pose now. Every breath, every class, I grow in flexibility and strength so that poses that once seemed impossible are suddenly accessible and realistic. Eventually they are even easy.

I used to struggle in Warrior Two to slide my front thigh into a parallel position. Now I step right into it. I used to struggle with squaring my hips in Warrior One. When the teacher would cue us to pull forward on the left hip and back on the right, in a right-foot-forward Warrior One, I'd think, "Okay, crazy lady." Now I slide right into place—strong, fierce, and facing forward.

Samara is three. Alan is two. I don't know then that this is the best it gets, that I will long for these days of young babies and endless park hours. I will miss the calls for Pirate's Booty (their favorite snack), and for grapes cut in fourths. I don't realize that girl drama and homework fights and sibling wars and heartbreak are just around the corner. I think this is the worst it can get, the hardest my life could be. The endless story requests and the hands on my body. The frustrating deadline days when Alan won't nap and Samara won't stop poking him.

The whole Warrior series becomes a mantra for my life. In Warrior One, our heels are aligned and our back heel is down. Our shoulders and hips square toward the front wall. We are strong and focused and forward-facing. Whatever challenges we face, we square hips. We square shoulders and face it head-on.

An angry editor, frustrating edits, a toddler meltdown: Breathe. Square. Face it. Confront it. Speak it.

In Warrior Two our arms are open. Our hips are open and facing the side wall. Our front heels are aligned with our back arches, and we are pulling the mat apart with our feet, through our strength. We are strong and open. We gaze over a finger steadily. We draw strength from our feet, pressing into the mat, and open our hips and our hearts. We are facing challenges with an open heart. This pose can be the most difficult. When we are in pain, our shoulders round, we pull in toward the center.

Grief, disappointment, and failure pull us in. People in grief cover their hearts, their eyes, their faces. Their shoulders pull forward. They hunch. They round their backs. They close their hearts. Why wouldn't they? But here we press our feet down. We open our hearts. It's okay. I may hurt again. I may even hurt worse. But it's worth it. I am strong. I am steady. I am grounded, dug into the earth that supports me.

Peaceful Warrior almost always follows Warrior Two. Physically it makes sense for the body. Flip the front palm, gaze steady. Tilt back. Follow the arm with the gaze. But it makes sense emotionally, too. After the courage it takes to remain open and strong, to keep my heart, mind, and gaze open to the possibilities, it's nice to find peace, to reassure myself that making myself vulnerable is the only road. This is the only way, the only choice.

In Warrior Three we each stand on one leg, toes pointed forward. The other leg extends behind, all five toes pointed down toward the earth. The hands can be at prayer. They can stretch out behind us, like wings. Or they can reach forward, Superman-like. It's a balance. The strength in this posture comes from the balance, from the heel pressing toward the back of the room and the crown reaching toward the front. I feel all four corners of the standing foot, rooting down, and then I reach, willing all my strength to the opposite ends of the room, with the rest of my body. In this pose everything comes together. There are so many different kinds of strength: open, fierce, balanced, and ready.

I walk out of the studio.

This is the beauty of yoga. Our bodies create a story and tell it again and again. In yoga training I will learn the real story of the Virabhadranasa (warrior) series. It's a story of grief and of the anger and destruction that comes from it. Lord Shiva marries Sati for love. Sati's father, King Daksha, disapproves of the marriage because Shiva was a little too much, with his dreadlocks and his skull companion (a skull he carries that is eventually fused to his body). When King Daksha fails to invite Shiva and Sati to a massive celebration, Sati grows full of rage, so much so that she burns herself to death. Shiva, in his fury, kills King Daksha with three moves: Warrior One, Warrior Two, and Warrior Three. King Daksha is beheaded by Shiva's sword. But the gory story has a happy ending. Daksha is brought back to life with the head of a goat after Lord Shiva takes pity on him. And Daksha sees all that Shiva has done and bows before him.

Violence and grief—it all makes sense. Symbolically, Shiva is the higher self, forever locked in a battle with the ego (Daksha), and all of it is for love (Sati). But for me it is the battle with the grief, the pain, and the longing.

I swing. I swing again, arms up and open, feet rooted to the earth.

"Where are you going, Mommy?" my ten-year-old Samara asks, her eyes filling with tears. She should know the answer. She sees the yoga mat on my back, the starburst-printed leggings, and the Uggs on my feet.

"Yoga," I answer, as I always do—because I always am.

The tears spill over.

"You are always going to yoga."

She's not wrong.

6. Balancing

IT ALL FLOWS BREATH TO BREATH HERE.
WE PRESS OUR FEET INTO THE MAT
AND STAND ON ONE FOOT,
CONFIDENT IN OUR ABILITY TO STAND
IN THE EYE OF THE STORM.

My Mother's Journals

I start reading my mother's journals by accident. The ones from her high school days are funny and enlightening, but in the way a fictional tale can be. They are not about a person I know and love. Although my mother is only in her late thirties when I start reading her journals, I view her high school days as Roman Empire–level history, and I don't see any harm in invading that privacy, especially since she has given me permission.

"Read them," she says. "They will make you laugh."

And they do. But they make me hungry for more. Once when I was way too young to be watching horror movies, a neighbor had Clive Barker's *Hellraiser* on. This terrifying tale is about a sexually deviant world traveler who receives a puzzle box from Hong Kong. When he opens it, he unleashes demons that rip him to shreds.

I didn't watch the whole movie, but I had gotten the gist of it. Maybe my mother's journals are like that puzzle box—something that looks benign and quiet that I should never touch, that will open up a world to me I'll wish I'd never known.

While my mother and my sister are out to lunch one day, I see a stack of notebooks in my mom's study. The green notebook from my childhood is there, along with maybe a hundred others, which fill the cubby: red, orange, blue, some with covers ripped off, some with bits of perforated paper sticking out through the wire spirals. Each notebook has been neatly labeled with a sharpie.

I open one marked "Kripalu, June 1983." The scrawl is familiar. My mother always writes in cursive. She once won awards for penmanship, and her writing is just the right size and slant, almost entirely legible. Some entries are in pencil and smudged, since this journal was written almost six years ago. But some are clear enough.

She talks about workshops and her meditation. *Just the chance to be silent is such a gift. Everything the guru says is something I want to learn more about.* This is life-changing for her. Her soul is awake, her creativity flowing. *I feel alive here.* Then I wonder, if she feels alive there, what does she feel at home?

I pick up another journal from July 1984. She is angry at my father, and her handwriting changes. She talks about the sacrifices she's made and how he wants another baby and she doesn't, and she says maybe she will leave both him and me to go live at the ashram. She repeats this page after page, day after day. The whole notebook is full of this anger and rage, a seething truth I have only partially seen.

He doesn't get me. We've grown apart. I wonder how I fit into this narrative. Do I not get her? These notebooks are full of secrets. Reading them will become a multiyear obsession, something I do every day.

I learn about her college boyfriend, Craig, the one she briefly left my father for. She talks about the sex with him and what that was like, and she talks about the sex with my father—page after page. Yuck.

This insight into my mother is fueling my adrenaline. My heart is pounding, and I feel like I've fallen into an undiscovered cave that just keeps going and going. I had no idea how angry she was. There is anger at her mother and her father, at her sisters, at my father—and at me. *Sasha is so selfish. She was so wonderful last night at the Passover seder, reading the four questions, but now I see her on the gymnastics floor, having a fit, acting like an asshole.*

Later I will learn that this is why people don't read other people's journals. It's best to give others their privacy because some things are better left unknown. I also learn that everyone needs a place to vent and that writing is better than speaking in this regard.

But I am shocked. She talks a lot about guilt, but I don't know why she feels so guilty. *The first time felt right. The second felt gratuitous.* What is she talking about? I start sifting through the books, flipping through pages. She is angry. She feels guilty. She loves traveling. Then I find the answer: She had two abortions, one when she was twenty and another when I was one. She talks about the guilt and the ambivalence. I think of all the prochoice marches she took me on and the canvassing we did for prochoice candidates. It seems like it should have been obvious, but it never was. Do I have dead siblings? Can I share this story?

I can never tell her I read the journal, but the secret is burning me up. I've always despised secrets. They feel like a lit match in my belly, scorching me from the inside. A few days later, when she is driving me across town to a friend's house, I do it. I ask.

"Did you ever have an abortion?"

She stiffens and grips the wheel tighter, her eyes on the road. If I hadn't been looking for it, I would have missed it. But then I wouldn't have asked the question, either. She doesn't answer. She's thinking. I know this silence. She's angry.

"Why would you ask that?"

"Because I want to know."

"Yes, but why would you even think of it?"

I am nervous. I imagine what she will say if I tell her. She will hide the journals, taking away my window into her thoughts. But more than that, she will know all that I know and have read and want to read, and that will change everything.

"It's just all that stuff you do, the rallies and envelope stuffing. I was wondering."

She is quiet a while as we pass through one side of town to another, but I can tell she is thinking.

I am thinking, too. When we lived in the city, my best friends from next door moved to Oakwood, a nicer neighborhood where the homes were older and had more character. The town would later come to be known primarily as the home of Brock Turner, the Stanford rapist who got a short sentence largely because he was white and so very "promising." But back then, during that summer, it was just "the other side of town," where my mother drove me every morning on her way to work as a therapist in an office near our old neighbors' new home.

We had full run of the neighborhood, with pools to swim in and submarine shops to walk to. We played dramatic games of tag and watched horror movies on the couch. We got in trouble daily. It was the most fun summer I ever had.

My friends have three children in their family. Josh, the oldest, is two years older than I am and is always involved in sports, music, or studying. He will become valedictorian of his Catholic high school and attend Yale. He stays in his room, avoiding the gaggle of girls running amuck through the chaperone-free house. Sarah is six months younger than I am, and we like to say we have been best friends since we shared a rattle on the playground at six months. I have no idea if this story is true, but we tell it all the time to anyone who will listen. Beth is the baby, even though she is only about eighteen months younger than I am. The three of us spend a lot of time squabbling over Nintendo controllers and who played Monopoly with whom last.

They are the reason I will have three children someday.

I was an only child until I was eight and a half. I remember their house being loud and wild, with children's toys filling the living room. Their father spent hours filming us with his new video camera, dancing to songs from the Madonna album *Like a Virgin* over and over again, with lace headbands and dangling earrings. It was a kid's house, the kind I wished I had.

In my house we've always watched news shows like *60 Minutes* or *The McNeil-Lehrer Report*. My toys and books and games are kept in my bedroom. My parents talk about Reagan at the dinner table, and I spend my free time stuffing envelopes at Planned Parenthood.

I am thinking of that loneliness, of being the only child in a highly adult-centered home. What would it have been like if my mother had had those two children?

I am angry. My arms are crossed over my skinny chest, still years from developing anything resembling an A cup. I slide down in the seat so the chest strap of the seat belt digs into my neck and the lap strap comes above my belly button.

"So what? Nothing? You have nothing to say?" I challenge my mother, watching a fly crawl from underneath the dashboard, across the radio, and to the air-conditioning blower near my right hand. I sit up and swat.

Bam! My hand hits the dashboard. I miss the fly, which buzzes past my ear. My mother is startled and looks at me, her mouth set in a straight line. Her eyes are narrow. I am in deep shit. She pulls the car over to the side of the busy road, and cars whiz by on her side. My mother's hands are still on the wheel.

"Sasha," she says.

Uh-oh.

"These are private, adult things. None of this is any of your business, and I don't have to share it with you. Abortion is private. It's between a woman and a doctor. It's none of your business."

She is repeating herself, and even though I am twelve, I know the political talking points about abortion all too well. She is repeating them as though we are at a campaign rally, not a mother and daughter having a conversation.

"But I feel like I need to know whether I would have had brothers and sisters. I feel like that *is* my business. I mean, should we have a funeral?"

She laughs, even though it's not funny. It's not an amused laugh. It's the kind of laugh that lets me know I am on very thin ice. Her temper is flaring. But I can't help myself.

"*Ahimsa* [nonviolence], Mom, right? Do no harm? Did you kill babies?"

She backhands my left shoulder. I clutch it, although I am stunned more than in pain. It's not the first time she's ever hit me, but it's the most unexpected. I struggle to find my breath.

She begins yelling. "This is none of your business. Abortion is private. Don't ask me this again."

I never do. She drives me to my friend's house and drops me off. She doesn't turn to look at me. She doesn't say good-bye. I get out of the car and walk into the house, hot tears spilling down my cheeks, but I don't turn back. I don't want her to see me cry.

A New Name

My mother goes on one last yoga retreat before starting chemotherapy. She's been a teacher for a couple of months, so the retreat provides a few days to sit quietly, to practice—the clichéd calm before the storm. This time she chooses a silent retreat.

She turned forty a few months ago. As she sits at Kripalu in her white linen, I imagine her noticing the changes in her body—not just from cancer, but the ones we all have as we age, when we realize that we won't always have the plump perfection of our youth to fall back on.

Her skin is growing thinner and more crepelike. She might notice the lines on her neck and be horrified by the loss of elasticity. The veins in her hands are starting to be more visible, and fine lines are creeping in around her eyes and mouth. But she still feels young. Forty is that kind of age—not really old, but old enough to understand she will be soon. At least she hopes so.

I am guessing these are the thoughts that fill her head as she pours crushed oats into a white porcelain bowl each morning, as she sprinkles cardamom, a bit of cinnamon, and some raisins on top. These are her thoughts as she places a tea bag in a porcelain cup and moves to the silent table where others, also in loose clothing, join her. She feels their energy but never hears their words. The only sounds are chewing and the occasional clink and clang of silverware, of spoons stirring honey into tea and forks scraping at scrambled tofu.

These five days are peaceful. "Just what I need," she writes in a letter to her sister, signing it "love, love, love! Susan."

Seventeen years from now I will tattoo these three words in her handwriting on my left wrist, but she doesn't know it then as she scratches her black pen against the legal pad, rips off the page, folds the paper, and sends it off to New York City, just three hours southeast of this beautiful place.

I tell people that my mother is away at a spa. It sounds better than the truth, and when I hear there is a world-class spa just one mile away from Kripalu, also in Lenox, I even use the name. "She's at Canyon Ranch," I tell my friends. "It's super fancy." It costs at least five times what Kripalu charges.

There is nothing luxurious about Kripalu. It's embarrassingly sparse. The only nod to luxury is a simple steam room, hot tub, and cold plunge pool, housed in a dingy basement, below the main dormitories and the cafeteria. Later, when I spend a few days here one summer, I entertain myself for hours by jumping into the cold pool, jumping out, shivering from my toes to my ears, and throwing myself back into the warmth of the swirling hot tub.

My mother doesn't like hot tubs. She gets massages, one luxury Kripalu offers in abundance. One every day. Bliss. But no pedicures, manicures, or beauty treatments of any kind—at least not yet.

This facility (founded by yogi Amrit Desai, aka Gurudev) is housed in a former Jesuit monastery, and it is an offshoot of Gurudev's original ashram in Pennsylvania. If Kripalu seems bare bones, the place in Pennsylvania is positively austere. My mother went there once, in 1982, and then switched her allegiance when the Massachusetts facility was built in 1983.

The focus at Kripalu is on what *feels* good, more than what *looks* good. There are bikes to rent, a lake nearby to swim in or skate on, miles of hiking trails, and a labyrinth in the back for contemplation. A shop sells mala beads, loose clothing, and books about chakras and crystals.

Gurudev has his own parking space, and for some reason, whenever we visit, my father finds this hilarious. Parking reserved for Gurudev. But every time he points it out, my mother asks the obvious. "What? Is he supposed to park at the lot half a mile away?"

"Why doesn't he ride a magic horse or like his mind's eye or something?" My dad looks at me as he asks this, nudging me into this mocking.

"Right, Sasha? Does *your* guru have a parking space?"

"I don't have a guru," I say.

No one is paying attention because my mother is too annoyed and my father is too far along this road. "I mean, a guru with a parking space. What a load. Does he drive a Mercedes?" Later we learn that he actually does. He lives in a small house within walking distance from the main building that the center built for him.

But this time—my mother's last retreat before starting chemo—my father and I are not there, which gives my mother plenty of time for walks in the woods and long rests on the expansive patio behind the main building, where she can nap and read her Dick Francis mysteries.

When she comes home, she has a new name.

"You can call me Kalyani," she tells me, as she walks into our living room. After five days away, she still looks the same: salt and pepper hair, big smile. But I am twelve, and I am having none of it. I am on the couch, feet propped up, a book open in front of me. I'd like to think I jumped up and gave her a hug, but I am sure I didn't. I just sat there, making her pay for her absence.

"Why don't I just call you Mom? And why would I call you Kalyani?"

She explains that they had to choose a Sanskrit name as part of the yoga teacher graduation, and she chose this one because it means good fortune.

"We can all use some of that," she says.

I wish I'd listened to her talk about this and asked her to tell me more, but instead I rolled over to my side and grunted something mocking. "Whatever, Kalyani."

She takes her bags and stands under our cathedral ceiling, her bare feet digging into the soft pile carpet that covers every floor in our house. She's looking at me. She is no martyr. She's pissed. I'm sure of it. I am sure her apathetic daughter's grunts and mocking are annoying, and when my mother gets mad she gives me the silent treatment for days at a time.

But this time I have the upper hand, and I know it. She feels guilty for her absence, for missing my track meet, for doing what she needed for herself. She stands there, staring, and I ignore her.

That night at the dinner table, my sister is yelling the lyrics to every song in *Cinderella*. Her bangs are in her eyes, and I glare at my mother.

See! See what happens in your absence? Your baby's hair is in her eyes. She's made bean chili, but I am not fooled. As I poke my spoon into the red mess of peppers and black beans and onions, small chunks of white float up.

"This has tofu. I am not eating this." I push it away. Tofu is a strict no-no for me, and she knows it. I find it gag-worthy. Any food with the consistency of cottage cheese, the look of a block of styrofoam, and the taste of silly putty is not anything I want as a meal. My mother has heard this before, and suddenly she's not so tranquil or yogic.

"I just got off a goddamn plane and took an hour making this. Eat it or eat nothing."

I push it away. "Fine. I'll starve. Awesome parenting."

She glares at me. My father, who is also looking at his bowl with some degree of disgust, brings up her new name.

"So what is Kalyani about?"

Even though the question sounds innocent, I wiggle in my seat in anticipation.

"It's my new name," she says, giving him a look.

"Your new name?" My father prods gently, but the smirk on his face gives away his game. We know he thinks it's silly, all this time she wastes on spiritual pursuits. He's a lawyer, a world traveler, a cultural Jew who let me stop Hebrew class when I was ten because I wanted to, and he knew it would spare him having to pay temple fees. We have been to synagogue only once as a family, and it was at my request.

My mother knows all this and gives him a look.

It's on.

My father's belly is pushing against the table. We have spent the week she was gone eating ribs and pork and bagels, piled high with cream cheese and lox and beefsteak tomatoes. My dad has blackened swordfish and grilled steaks. He's made a pot of chocolate and a sugar-loaded Cincinnati chili served over pounds of white pasta.

None of us want the vegetarian chili my mother has made. I look down at my bowl and watch as the small chunks break apart and float to the surface. It's like egg drop soup, if egg drop soup tasted like the bottom of a dirty foot.

"Yes, Ashley. My new name."

I can tell she's tired of explaining this again and again. It's loud in our house, and my sister is making it louder. Clang! Her spoon bangs against the table. Clang! Again. She sticks her hand in the chili bowl and smears some red sauce on her face, digging out the tofu bits.

"Just take it out if you don't like it," Mariel explains. "See, it's easy." She drops the chunk of tofu next to the plate. Easy. Sure.

"So what does it mean?" my dad asks.

"It means good fortune."

"And you want us to call you that?"

"No," she says, a look of shame crossing her face. "I mean, only when I am teaching."

I get it now, as an adult, about the name. It's like Sara and Sasha. It's the name that makes her feel strong, able to fight the cancer, able to take it on. But I don't get it then, when I'm a kid, so I laugh at her, and so does my father.

"Can we give you a nickname?" he asks. "Like, can we call you Kali or Yani or Kal?"

We think this is hilarious. My mother looks at us, her jaw tight. Surely she is practicing ahimsa now. This is nonviolence, the first yama. The yamas are a set of rules and commandments yogis have for living. Ahimsa is the first. We do no harm—to animals or people. Although my mother isn't discussing any yamas now, she's certainly considering this one. I watch her fists form into balls. Ahimsa is why we have tofu in our bowls instead of animal flesh. Ahimsa is why she is refraining from punching us all.

Thank God for ahimsa!

She looks at us and shakes her head. My dad is still chuckling. I hammer the final nail. "I mean, I'm just saying, I liked it better when Dad made us burgers. That's all."

She nods. "Okay, tomorrow we do takeout."

Her wooden chair squeaks as she gets up and moves it across the brown tile, which she and my father chose five years ago as they were building this house. They called it earthy. It reminds my mother of Santa Fe, as do all the Gorman paintings of Native Americans scattered around the house, strategically positioned under earthen sconces and hanging chili peppers.

"I am going to bed," she says, seething with white hot anger.

My dad, ever ready to poke, can't resist. "It's seven PM."

This is annoying, because going to bed early is his favorite activity. She ignores him and marches up the stairs. We hear the door slam, and I look at my dad, reaching across my sister to pull a chunk from a loaf of French bread in the center of the table. I take a bite of the chunk, and the crust falls on my chest.

"What'd I say?" I wonder aloud, brushing the crumbs onto the floor. "Dad, can we order a pizza?"

More Secrets and Balcony Jumping

We don't burn the journals after my mother dies. My father piles them into boxes, like the porn he once kept in my closet, and puts them in his bedroom closet. When we move to the new house in Boston, he puts them somewhere else, and I never quite find them. When we move for the last time, while I am in college, he places them high on a shelf in the garage.

He doesn't know that I have read them all, but each one is as familiar to me as my own notebooks: the Ramona Quimby friendship journal, the silk-covered journal my father brings me home from a business trip in China, the cat notebook with quotes about kittens on every page, and the journal with quotes about friendship. I fill them with my stories as quickly as she filled hers.

While she was alive, I would sneak in her room to read them when she wasn't looking. To be fair, she would barely hide them. They'd be beside the computer where I played Oregon Train and Lemonade Stand. They'd be sitting on the edge of her bed while she took a bath and yelled to me through the door. I longed to know her personal thoughts, her mysteries.

Snooping is my game as a child. I perfect the art of holding down the button on the phone as I pick up the receiver to listen to my parents' secret conversations. They are vaguely sexual, always confusing. What does inside mean? Is that like a dollhouse? I listen to my mother talk to her friends. I rifle through file cabinets. For most of my life I believe that this desire to know, to find out, and to be aware comes from my mother's silence and her mysterious nature and secrets. Lately I've started to wonder if it was loneliness that drove my curiosity. For the first nine years of my life there was nothing to distract me from the secrets of my parents, no one else in the house to be curious about.

My mother's journals are full of anger, regret, and secret desires: to be a writer, to live in a different town, to leave my father. It scares me. She says that my father's constant travel and his disdain for her spiritual path make them incompatible. Will she go?

They kiss in the kitchen later, holding each other tight, making out. I am repulsed but also relieved. Okay. She wrote it, but she didn't mean it.

It will take me years to understand the truth about journals. We say the unspeakable there so we can be more present in our daily lives.

In my adult life, I have learned not to excavate my mother's emotional landscape. Each new thing—the college boyfriend, the dips in and out of an open marriage, the pregnancies—feel like an aha moment. I know who she is now. I can stop. I have finally uncovered the mystery: why she locks her bedroom door at night when my father is out of town; why I sometimes hear her cry.

But I never find the bottom. There is always more to know. I keep digging to find what she is really thinking, behind the Buddha-on-the-mountaintop approach she sometimes takes to life. But all I get when I ask her anything is a smile, a hand on the shoulder, or a gentle kiss on the forehead. That's it?

Of course, when she loses it, she really loses it. Then I get a slap or the grab of an arm. On the day she catches me and several friends throwing ourselves from the second-floor balcony onto a pile of couch cushions below, she grabs me by the arm. "How could you be so stupid? If those kids hurt themselves, we'd pay. Do you know that? Do you care?" She shakes me by the shoulders and shoves me back.

My father intervenes. "Take a breather," he tells her.

He looks at me.

"I think she'll kill me," I say.

But she doesn't. We just go on. That night she writes in her journal that she is sorry, that she lost control, and that she will not do this the next time. Being a mother is hard. I will understand this sixteen years from now, fourteen years after she's gone, when I feel my own hands tighten around my daughter's shoulders as she tests me.

"You are the worst mom ever. I hate you."

There it is: that disappointment, that disdain and disrespect. I can feel my fingers tighten. Now I know how my mother felt. This is what she went through. I see my hands on my mat, with the veins showing, as I stare at the space beneath my fingernails, white with my grip—as they are here, on my daughter's birdlike shoulders, the thumbs digging in. The pads of my fingers could so easily bruise her.

Sometimes, if I stay mindful, I remember the regret my mother felt afterward. *I'll never do that again.* I let go—sometimes, not always.

None of my friends got hurt when we jumped off the balcony.

Marcus was the only one who wore shoes, so he left a long scuff mark on the white balcony. We all heard the scrape when it happened. "How will I ever explain that?" I asked. Marcus laughed, his face in the pillows, an overweight kid with wire-framed glasses who reminded all of us more than a little of Piggie from *Lord of the Flies*.

The long black streak of a scuff mark remains, long after my mother dies. It is there when we sell the house. Every time I see it I think of my mother.

"How could you? How could you?" my mother screams when she finds us jumping.

How could I?

Her journals are to her what my yoga will be to me. I like it in the hottest room possible. I like to hold Utkatasana (chair) until my legs feel numb and my shoulders ache. I breathe. I find the gaze. I pull up on the muscles for urination and in the low belly. My *bandhas*, my inner strength, is what keeps me lifted. In hot yoga, the sweat drips and burns and sometimes blinds.

I am playing with discomfort on my mat so I can deal with what happens off the mat as well. My mother was expressing the worst of herself and locking the door to me so she could be her best with me later, when it mattered. "How was your day? Did you take care of yourself?" she would ask.

When I am in my late thirties my father finds out that I have read my mother's journals. He asks if I regret reading them and knowing what I know. He refuses to show them to my sister, worried that the few memories she has will be tainted. I regret invading my mother's privacy, being a silly twelve-year-old, and leaping from the balcony because now, with three kids of my own, I can feel every shrieking second: the terror of liability, of broken bones, and of horrible calls to the parents of all the other children who have done incredibly stupid things they regret.

Then they learn. What more can we ask?

There is a danger every day of turning a dead woman into a saint, of making my mother into someone with no flaws, no downside, and no dark secrets. This could strip her of her humanity, of the very thing that makes her interesting and compelling, even twenty-four years after her death. I am still chasing her ghost, and it's not because she was a perfect human or mother.

"Everything I did led here," I tell my father. "This life. My children. This path. This love." To focus on the mistakes we made, the many near misses, is to lose the thread that got us here in the first place. Who would I have become if I hadn't snooped? Who would she be for me?

Becoming a Woman, Part One

"What will happen when my period comes?" Samara is nearly eleven. Her questions start coming rapid-fire fast after the fourth-grade puberty assembly. I get a copy of Judy Blume's puberty classic, *Are You There, God? It's Me, Margaret* and hope that Samara will love it as much as I did. She doesn't.

I am not even sure she's read it. Rob and I exchange glances. We are driving to the gym; her brother is home alone, and her sister is still at school. For parents of three kids, having moments alone together with any one of them is so rare. And now this.

"There will be blood. You will have to find a way to catch it."

"Will I use tampons?"

"Yes, at some point. But maybe not right away. It depends when you get it."

"When will I get it?"

"I don't know. No one can tell you that."

I tell her that when she does get it, we will do something special. I imagine a trip to Mexico or some kind of ceremony. Welcome to womanhood. I imagine red tents and other women there to advise and guide.

"When did you get it?" she asks.

"Old. I was old. Much older than you."

7. Strengthening

EVERYTHING BUILDS TO THIS MOMENT
OF FIRE—THE LONG HOLD.
FOR A TEACHER, THIS IS WHERE WE GET
STUDENTS UNCOMFORTABLE.
WE WANT TO SEE THEM BREAK THE POSE
AND COME BACK INTO IT.
THIS IS WHERE WE BUILD ALL THE STRENGTH.

Easter Tornado and the Last Photo of My Mom

The last photo I have of my mother is one she didn't want me to take. "I can't stand it if you remember me this way," she says, as if I would ever forget, as if the memory of her bald head, confused eyes, and birdlike frailty would ever be far from my psyche.

The photo is taken after dinner, just before bed. I take it because she is in the adjustable bed in her study and can't get out. She can protest, but she can't really stop me, and I want a photo of her. It's not because I want to remember this moment. I will spend the rest of my life wishing I could forget it. But I need proof: the scar and the pain were real. And here's why I need proof. When they see the photo, they will know. I have no idea who "they" is.

My mother is pale. Her head sits like a lollipop on top of her skeletal body. Every bone is prominent. Her collarbone juts from her chest and creates a crevice so deep we joke that a small mammal could take a bath there. Her wrists had always been delicate, but now they are frail, so small that my seven-year-old sister can encircle them with her thumb and forefinger.

My mother is bald. "Like an egg," she had joked when the hair first came out, but we don't joke anymore, not about anything. We are nearing the end. Even going into the living room requires a wheelchair and moans of pain.

I invite my friend Angela over for the night, and she sits on the edge of my bed, legs tense, eyes wide. "Is it always like this?" she asks. "Does she always moan?"

I am surprised because I'd hardly noticed. The constant, rhythmic moans of pain have become the soundtrack to my life. They stop only when she has morphine.

This is how I convince her to let me take the photo. I am in my pajamas, an outfit I put together and find impossibly cool in that mid-1990s grunge sort of way. It consists of a pair of white long underwear, a baggy pair of flannel shorts over that, and an oversized Georgetown sweatshirt—not because I have any connection to the school, but because the sweatshirt was on sale and I could cut the collar off to make it look even more distressed.

The first two photos I take are just of my mother. She doesn't smile. She's in a soft pink T-shirt and has a scarf wrapped around her head. It's a scene from a Monet painting, something in soft blues and greens. The pastel colors contrast so much with the chemo port, visible beneath her shirt; the sharp cut of her elbows; and the fierce edge of the tendons now visibly angry in her wrists and forearms. But the pastels remind me of a memory, something I'd filed away long ago and forgotten.

"Do you remember the Easter tornado?" I ask. My mother's favorite holiday is Easter. I prefer Halloween, with the macabre darkness in the crisp fall air, and the candy and the opportunity to be someone else, even if only for a single night. I spend all year planning my costume and incorporating a theme. My sister loves Christmas because of Santa and presents, and Chanukah because of more presents.

It's always been Easter for my mother. She loves the new life of spring, with the buds on the trees and the creepiness of a giant bunny inexplicably delivering chocolate and pastel-colored eggs to children as they sleep. I also think she loves the togetherness of it.

We always do Halloween alone at our house with just my friends and local neighborhood kids. We do both Christmas and Chanukah with family, but it's always too big, too overwhelming, and too stressful. People fly into Cleveland whom we have to see all at once. There is baking, cooking, wrapping, the fear of impending snowstorms, and the stress of getting everything done in time.

Easter is quiet, a celebration of renewal and rebirth without the hassle of the winter holidays. We always spend it in Cleveland with my mother's family. My Aunt Lu always makes a lamb cake, a coconut-covered treat in the shape of a lamb with Easter eggs in its hooves: mint green, pink, light blue. My grandmother bakes a ham. Only my mother's siblings come over. There is no extended family drama or cousins to argue with or who drink too much. There is no ice on the road or a miserable dad to contend with. As a Jew who never celebrated Christmas as a kid, my father hates Christmas. He hates the pageantry of it all, the obligations, and the way it made him feel like a child: lonely, unwanted, and on the outside. He's neutral on Easter, though.

The memory of this particular Easter is vague and shaky. I must have been two or three, and the windows rattled and then broke. Tornado sirens went off, and I heard the sound of Bampa screaming.

"Tornado?" My mother asks me this now.

At the time she threw herself on top of me and pinned me down, but I didn't feel squashed or scared. I felt safe and protected, as though my mother would protect me despite my small size. Her lioness instinct would keep me from harm. I barely remember the details, but I do remember the feeling. I remind her of this natural disaster we experienced on Easter.

She squints her eyes. The cancer has spread to her brain. Her memory is fuzzy. She forgets words, dates, and people's names. She is blind in her left eye from the metastatic cells. They sit on the part of her brain that controls her sight. She can no longer read books.

"I don't think that happened," she says later.

It did. I swear it did.

In the rush of all that comes later—her pain, her death, and our move—I forget about the Easter tornado. I forget to ask Nana about it. I forget to ask Bampa. It's on a car drive nearly twenty years later, alongside my husband, that I will suddenly pull out my iPhone and Google the tornado in Cleveland on April 8, 1980, when I was two.

"It was a Tuesday," Rob points out, looking over my shoulder.

So it is. I Google again. Easter Sunday was April 6. We had stayed a few days after. My two-year-old brain had conflated the two. But it happened. I am vindicated. I wish I could call my mother. *See? I remember. I was right.*

She and I argue about it again. I insist I remember the glass breaking and being underneath her, confident in her ability to protect me from anything. I need her to remember because of this. She is strong. She is invincible. Has she forgotten? Has the cancer made her forget she hiked up to Machu Picchu? That she can stand on her head for half an hour at a time? That only she can protect me from broken glass, ripping wind, and funnel clouds? They suck everything up into their center and spit them back out, broken and destroyed. But not me. Because I have her.

"That never happened," she says again. "Never."

There is no one to confirm or deny. No Google I could use in 1993. She's agitated. Her sister comes in. "You need to leave," she tells me. The gatekeeper, always.

I give up on the tornado and ask my aunt for a favor. "Can you take a photo before I go? Just one?"

She nods in that clipped way she has. She looks like my mother physically, but the likeness ends there. She is all hard edges and mean observations. She can take your breath away with her cruelty. Today is no different. She is obviously annoyed and in a hurry, far more concerned with her sister than her sixteen-year-old niece.

I climb into bed with my mother and hug her against me. Her bones feel sharp. I can feel each one hard against my hands. She grimaces. "Not so tight." I was squeezing too hard. I release her a bit but tilt my head toward her. Her sister takes the photo and shoos me out the door. I take the camera back and start to leave.

"I love you, Mom," I whisper. She doesn't hear me.

I develop the photos two weeks after she dies. I am a giantess beside her. I am a size four, but I look enormous next to her, almost puffy, like a marshmallow Peep over a flame. My cheeks are round and ruddy. Hers are sunken and hollow. But she's trying to smile and look like it's all okay. She's protecting me still.

Even if she forgets, I remember.

Icelandic Cape

We are getting rid of my mother's things. She'd be so proud. She loved to purge. She'd pile up giant boxes full of papers, art projects, and old report cards, and to the curb it would go.

"Mom, where is my shirt [or pants, homework, or shoes]?" I always knew that whatever it was, I could find it on the curb, being returned to the universe, as she would always say. We gave my mother back to the universe a few weeks ago, and now we have to throw out her clothing.

"Do you want this?" My father is holding up a cape, wool and shaggy with the black outline of something amorphous and sheep-like. Obviously, no. My friends and I will later pour amaretto sours at Leah's house and laugh. *Icelandic cape? What kind of idiot wears an Icelandic cape?*

My dad looks up at me from the floor and all that is left of my mother. "We bought that on our trip to Iceland. She loved it." I know that trip. They'd been on a budget of five dollars a day for two summers, backpacking through Europe. Flying through Reykjavik was the cheapest way to mainland Europe. They spent a few days exploring the fjords.

It will be years before I go there with my husband and we fall in love with the land of fire and ice. We will take a camper around the ring road with our three children. The camper will get stuck in ice. We will have to walk miles to get help. We will fight on black-sand beaches and be the only humans we see for days. I will wish I had my mother's Icelandic cape. I wish I could tell her now that I know who wears one.

My dad throws the cape on the trash pile. I mostly want nothing: Not her mala beads or crystals. Not her bird pin or wedding ring. I don't want the heels she wore in the 1970s or the knee-high boots. I do want her curlers, but that's only because my own set broke. I also want her car, the blue Geo Prism I will cover with stickers inside and out.

My mother leaves a note, but it doesn't mention my father, my sister, or me. It is addressed to her parents and siblings, her "first family." She leaves them mirrors and pictures and a meditation pillow. She leaves us nothing.

"It must have been too hard for her," my grandmother and my aunts tell me. They don't seem to know that it's hard for me, too, to have nothing: No note. No sign. She promised, but she left nothing.

My grandmother dreams of her. "She's on her mat. She's doing yoga. She's not in pain, and she has hair."

Why her? I wonder. *Why not me? Why can't I see her?* I must not have been spiritual enough. My mother must have known.

"What about this?" my father asks. He's holding up my mother's black yoga mat, rolled up inside a tie-dyed carrier, but I know exactly what it is. I wish I could reach back in time and shake that sixteen-year-old girl. I wish I could tell her it's the one thing she will want most. But I don't. My father puts the malas and crystals in a safe spot.

He puts the jewelry I reject in a box in his drawer. He saves the earrings and bird pin. The mat goes in the trash.

Never again will I practice yoga, I tell myself.

She wanted to be cremated. She wanted all the journals burned. She wanted a tree planted at her ashram and her ashes scattered there. But that isn't what happens.

She *is* cremated. Each member of the family spends a few minutes alone with her, one at a time, before the undertakers take her body away: my grandmother, my aunt, Bampa, and my sister, who arrives at hospice a couple of hours after I do.

Her skin is cold, like a porcelain doll. Within seconds I want to leave the room. My hands shake. I am sweating. My feet are tingling with the urge to run. I want to fling open the door and bolt outside on this cold November day and scream at the sky to fuck off.

This is a perfect day to die: November 17, 1993. It's the time of year when everything turns cold and dies, when the trees shed their final leaves, and the few that straggle behind look like skeletons, dark brown and crunchy, holding on in a futile attempt to change the inevitable.

Many years later, when I am teaching yoga, I will hold my students in Utkatasana, the chair pose. I will tell them to place their weight on their heels and reach their arms long overhead, to engage the fingertips as though they could shoot fire into the sky, to lift their gaze between their thumbs, to try to expose the heart, to soften the shoulder, and to tilt the pelvis. Then I will tell them to sink another inch because we grow the most in the times we hurt, when we shake and sweat and pour.

But being at my mother's deathbed is not a moment of growth. I am paralyzed with discomfort and fear. I only know that I don't want to stand in this room, breathing the same air that she died in. It's stale, and her face is pale. This person has the same high cheekbones my mother did, the same soft and wide lips. But she is not my mother because my mother isn't dead.

I would tell a student in a difficult pose to breathe into the pain, to learn to recognize the difference between discomfort and genuine pain from injury, and to lean into the growth—to hold the truth in your hand in front of your face and not let it go until it's shown you what it needs to show you. The yoga pose is never about the pose or the way we grow stronger physically by holding it. It's about what happens to the body and the mind. It's about building a strong foundation of breath and presence.

But none of this knowledge is available to me at my mother's deathbed, and the person who knows it is dead. I cry because I know I am supposed to, but I am numb. Tomorrow I will tell my mom all about this bizarre day: how cold she felt, that I saw a dead body for the first time, and that it was my mom. And then I remember that there *is* no tomorrow, that my mother will never have one, and this is the last time I will see her.

I would tell my students to feel grounded in all points of contact and to remember they are safe and loved. They are breath and light.

But nothing feels right or safe. Nothing feels grounded at all.

Two weeks later my mother comes back to us in a box. It's made from oak, big and thick and heavy, and none of us open it because no one wants to see the color of the ashes, the bits of bone and whatever else remains after everything burns.

A gold plaque bears her name: Susan Schaefer Brown. Before she was married she was Susan-Jo, but she dropped the Jo when she took Brown. My father always called her Susan-Jo. It should really say that on the plaque because I don't think we will remember her any other way. She's already fading away: the sound of her laugh, the temperature of her skin, the way her fingers felt on my hair when I put my head in her lap.

Now it's all ash and dust.

In the spring we will take these ashes to the ashram and bury them beside the tree. It makes sense because in a few months our family will move to Boston, which is just a couple of hours from the Berkshires. As I remember this, I also recall that "family" means three now: me, my sister, and my dad. That's it.

My grandparents don't agree with our decision to cremate, but it is what my mother wanted. They want the ashes in Cleveland so they can be close to them. We agree to give them half. It feels weird to divide the ashes. I watch as they sift their fingers through my mother's ashes, but I don't get close enough to see anything. I can't look. It feels exposed and wrong, like someone reaching under my skirt and grabbing wherever he can.

My grandparents put their half of the ashes in a zip-lock freezer bag so they can place part of their grown daughter beside their baby who died at birth forty-seven years ago.

"God wanted my first baby," Nana tells me.

I wonder if she's right, if there was a decision made early in my grandmother's life that the firstborn would be taken, and when the second born moved up in line, she would die, too. Isn't that a bad sign, a curse, or karma?

I look at Nana and wonder how she pissed off God so much, if it was her genes that gave my mother the cancer, and if her karma killed both of her girls. If so, it couldn't possibly be my karma.

First Pregnancy and Yoga

Yoga goes in and out of my life during my early years in Boston. I buy monthlong passes to Baptiste, and some months I practice every day. Then I don't practice at all for long stretches. I run and run, then an injury sidelines me, and I think: *Yoga. I should try that again.*

I am not planning to get pregnant. But I go off the pill because it is giving me mood swings, discomfort, and bloating. Rob and I have been married three years, so it makes sense. A baby? Not yet, he says. We have too much left to do. We are only twenty-eight. But we aren't careful just one time, which is all it takes.

I take a pregnancy test alone in the bathroom, but I am up before the pee dries. Rob is standing outside. There are two lines. I scream it. I shout it. Two lines. I take another test, and another. I keep coming up with two lines. So there it is. I am pregnant.

Right away I want to be perfect. I want to do everything right. I cut out processed food, sodium, and ice cream. I buy a cookbook and start making salmon cakes by hand. Salmon cakes! I carefully chop each red pepper and green onion. I sprinkle whole-grain bread crumbs into the mix. I shape each salmon cake as though it is all that stands between my baby and Harvard. A gentle pat makes a perfectly round patty. I focus on every vitamin, mineral, and SAT point my baby will need to catapult out of my womb directly into the Ivy League.

Within a week I am vomiting. It's not morning sickness, though. It's a stomach bug, a high fever that sends me to the hospital multiple times. Will my baby be okay? What does a fever do? It's early, the doctor tells me. Go home. Rest. I do, but I can't.

I get better, but I worry. I ask my doctor what I can do. Are you exercising? she asks. All the new research shows that exercise is a great way to keep baby weight-gain low, between fifteen and twenty-five pounds. I've given up the running I so loved because I'd never forgive myself if the baby were jostled and had shaken baby syndrome or if he or she fell out of the warm, safe sac into my underwear because I attempted to run seven miles.

My doctor laughs. I will eventually switch from a doctor to a midwife because of this laugh, and because she tells me there is a Cesarean section rate of 75 percent. "You will never be able to have a natural birth," she says. "Everyone says they want a natural birth. No one gets one."

That laugh. Right now she is still my doctor, and she offers me the best possible advice. What about yoga? I ask. By now my image of yoga has morphed from the gentle, mindful, horrifically boring and dull practice of my childhood into the hot, sweaty, incredibly physical practice I have done in a 104-degree room at Baptiste. How could that be good for a baby? She laughs. That damn laugh again. But this time it makes sense: Not hot yoga, she says. Look for a prenatal class.

I do. I live in one of those gentrifying towns that keep popping up around major cities as metropolitan areas become too expensive for hipsters and artists: Brooklyn in New York, Silver Lake in Los Angeles, Fountain Square in Chicago. And Somerville in Boston.

The town that was once called Slummerville is now home to multiple vegan bakeries, at least two dog parks, a movie theater with midnight showings of 1970s B-grade horror films, and an artisanal doughnut shop that serves bacon on top of maple-glazed fried dough. The town is also rife with $1,000 strollers, handlebar mustaches, and at least ten unicycles.

On the outskirts of town is a little maternity shop called Isis. It's exactly the kind of place that belongs near a town full of married hipsters in their late twenties and early thirties. It's part gift shop, part community center, part education center, part Gymboree, and part clothing store.

Rob and I walk from our condo down a long stretch of Massachusetts Avenue that takes us past dance studios, Mexican restaurants, laundromats, and a church. The logo of the maternity shop is a purple monkey with round eyes, holding its baby. "We are home," I tell Rob.

Inside, the gear is what all hipster parents dream of owning, such as a $150 baby carrier and a $100 nursing bra that completely covers the belly. We buy the first two gifts we will ever buy for our baby: a cardboard copy of *Urban Babies Wear Black* and a Sandra Boynton book that makes us laugh out loud. If we still laugh at board books, are we really prepared to be parents?

The shop offers prenatal yoga, three times a week, eighteen dollars a pop. I buy a class card. "Put your hand on your belly and send your baby warm thoughts," the teacher says. We are in a quiet room with a thick carpet. We are given thick, padded mats very different from the ones we used to practice on at Baptiste, which were practically as thin as a sheet of paper. The lighting in the room is dim, and each corner has one of those flickering lights designed to look and move like a candle without the liability of a real flame.

The teacher is impossibly beautiful. She tells us she has three kids, but I can't imagine how any of them grew inside her tiny, taut body. I am in that phase at the beginning of pregnancy where it just looks like I've been eating too many doughnuts. She has a "six-pack," a series of perfect abs layered one on top of the other. She wears her blond hair in long dreadlocks and has colored tattoos all over her arms: the *om* sign; a peace sign; a vine of green leaves crawling up her outer arm and twisting around to her shoulder. I never learn her name, so I call her Ivy.

I decide that after this baby comes, I will look like Ivy. Never mind that I didn't look like Ivy before having a baby. At this point anything seems possible.

We start to breathe. I am by far the woman in the earliest stage of pregnancy. We go around and tell our stories. "I am Sasha. I am eight weeks pregnant with my first. I don't know if it's a girl or a boy, and I am delivering at Newton-Wellesley Hospital."

Two moms are overdue by a week. The woman to my right, Mary, has long brown hair and a belly straining against her maternity shirt. I am fascinated by her belly button, which looks like a button on a turkey popping to indicate doneness. Yet here she sits.

"Maybe this class will help," Mary says. "Lord knows nothing else has."

Ivy smiles. She walks over to Mary and places her face an inch from her belly. "Come out, beautiful boy. We all want to meet you." Her voice is melodic and hypnotic, the kind of voice that makes me want to lie down and stroke my shoulders. She sounds like my mother.

"Everyone come and lie on your left side," she tells us. We all oblige. She tells us to put one hand on our bellies and the other on our hearts. My belly hasn't even popped. My right hand is flat on my skin. I try to imagine what's inside—a zygote, a long strange head, more Gumby than human.

"Hello, in there. It's Mommy." *How weird. How can I be someone's mommy?*

"Say hello, baby," Ivy tells my belly.

I've spent my whole life being told this entity is a fetus, but now it's a baby. How strange. But I go with it because this baby is so wanted, so beloved and exalted.

Ivy is on her hands and knees, moving her hips. "Lubricate those hips, ladies." We do—bellies pointed down, hips sinking back to heels. We are relaxing to Ivy's sweet, melodic voice. It's heaven.

I am still in shape from my previous workout schedule, so this class feels slow and painful. It's more about breath and belly rubs than a workout. Ivy holds us in the Child pose and encourages us to do Kegel exercises.

"Pull up on the muscles of urination like you are going up an elevator, one floor at a time. Then release at the same time."

"Why are we doing this?" I ask.

"Strong muscles open more easily."

Ah.

I do my Kegels. I wonder what will happen to my abs. I imagine this baby growing and spreading, my skin stretching and accommodating. None of it feels possible. I will never look like Ivy. I look down at my belly while I am in the Tadasana (mountain) pose. It is still mostly flat. How strange to have new life. How odd it all is.

"Next Wednesday night, ladies," Ivy says, as we file out. I know I will be there.

From that moment on, I never miss a class with Ivy—Wednesday night, Sunday morning. We do Kegels. We do supported lunges and stretches. We use the blocks, the blankets, the bolsters, and the straps—all the tools and modifications I would have scoffed at before the baby. It's a careful practice, one that takes into account our joints and the change in our center of gravity. Balance poses are done against the wall. We do a lot more low lunging than high lunging. Home base is Tabletop rather than Downward Dog.

It is Ivy (and yoga) who finally encourages me to go another direction with my birth. She recommends her midwife practice. They deliver babies at the same hospital at which I'd planned to deliver, but their C-section rate is less than 10 percent, and they are holistic in their approach.

"I never could have avoided the epidural if I hadn't gone with the midwife," Ivy notes. She recommends her hypnobirthing coach, too. "It jives so well with yoga."

Hypnobirthing is all about the use of visualization, breath, and self-hypnosis to help the body unfold and open and allow the baby to pass through. Rob and I attend four weekly sessions of hypnobirthing and then hire the coach to help us privately as we get further into the third trimester.

"We are such cliché yuppy parents," Rob says.

I don't care because, even if we are, I have to find my place. Other women have mothers. They have aunts and cousins and generations of women who can help them through labor and delivery. At least I imagine they do. If my mother were here, she'd have words of wisdom. After all, she'd delivered both my sister and me, without drugs. I was in the room when my sister came out, purple and puffy, covered in waxy white vernix, screaming as if she'd been poked with a cattle prod.

My parents thought I'd do well being in the room. They believed that my being part of the birth process would make becoming a sibling at age eight a bit easier. I watched my mother writhe, scream, bleed, and beg. I watched her claw the bed, her knuckles white and drawn. "Oh God," she moaned. "Oh God."

I wondered if she would die, if anyone could survive this seeming tsunami of pain and torture. Why should it be this way? She paced the halls. She gritted her teeth. She clawed my father's shoulder. Yet when the time came, and Mariel was out and wrapped in a flannel receiving blanket, all pink and perfect, my mother pressed her index finger into the dimple on her chin. "Hello, my beautiful baby. Hello, my beautiful you."

I knew then, even at eight, that I could do it, too, that this is what motherhood was: the natural disaster, the earthquake, the hurricane, the tidal wave of pain and twisted terror—and then calm, love, the 100 percent sure bet that it was all worth it, in spite of every surge and white-knuckled scream. It brought us closer to the *samadhi* of this perfect moment: all love, all calm, all life.

So I do what she did: yoga. I practice twice a week with Ivy. As my belly grows, poses that used to feel absurdly easy now feel difficult, challenging, and almost impossible. I am short of breath and have to work harder to find the deep inhalations and equal exhalations. The Savasana pose that felt too long to hold early in my pregnancy becomes too short by week thirty-six. Only ten minutes? Are you kidding?

I imagine Ivy's life. She lives in Somerville, of course. She grows all her own food. Each one of her blond and apparently perfect children is smarter than the last. They wear sweaters she knitted herself from wool she bought in Norway (because we are still in the phase of parenthood where everything we covet is made in Scandinavia). Her round light-wood crib costs $800. The stroller runs about $1,500, depending on the model. The adjustable high chair made of dark walnut is only $400.

I am certain Ivy has it all and that I will never live up to any of it. But no matter how inadequate Ivy makes me feel in ab definition and holistic lifestyle, she more than makes up for it in class. "Breathe in love for your baby. Exhale love for the world. It's all the same. Love the baby as you love the world."

With Ivy and yoga, I think, I am pretty sure I can shape this world exactly as I want it to be. This baby will be born into so much love and compassion and adoration that no natural disaster—not SIDS, not choking, not cancer—could ever come between us.

This baby will be safe. And because she is safe, I will be, too.

8. surrendering

A FIVE- TO TEN-MINUTE HOLD OF A YIN POSTURE,
WHICH DEEPLY SURRENDERS AND
STRETCHES THE BODY
AND MIGHT INCLUDE BACKBENDS OR HEART OPENERS
THAT HELP US GET VULNERABLE AND GOOEY.

Spider in a Jar— First Time

A black spider is crawling up the wall. "He's looking at me!," I scream when I see it. "Agh! Oh my God, Jesus, fuck!" We swear a lot in my house, especially when spiders are involved.

My mother comes running up the stairs. "This is why you called me up here? A spider? Jesus. I thought someone broke into the house," she says. She's been washing dishes downstairs, and I hear the water draining in the sink.

My sister walks out from the bedroom, a handful of pink "girl" Legos in her hand.

"What's happening?" she asks. Mom scoops her up in her arms and kisses her cheek.

I point to the spider. "See? Fucking see?" I demand. My sister gasps.

"Don't say that word," my mother says, but that's for my sister's benefit, and no one is paying attention. We are all looking at the giant black spider that has barely moved since I spotted it. Later, I will tell people it was as big as my hand or possibly larger. I will also say that it was hairy, spotted, and almost certainly poisonous. None of this is true, however. It is maybe half the size of my hand.

My mother is terrified of spiders. She likes to pretend otherwise because being afraid of creepy-crawlies doesn't fit the image she has crafted of a nature-loving yogi. That image may be true, but she still hates spiders. She has squashed them for years. Actually, my father squashes them while my mother screams and runs away.

A spider once dropped from a silky white web onto my mother's shoulder, and she ran out of the house screaming, as if a serial killer were after her with a machete.

Thanks to her example, my sister and I both suffer from crippling arachnophobia. I have nightmares of spiders crawling in my mouth. I read somewhere that every human, statistically speaking, has eaten at least three spiders in his or her sleep. I considered taping my mouth shut with duct tape each night as a means to deny that fate.

"Get a jar," my mother tells my sister, who runs down to the kitchen. My mother and I silently watch the spider, sure that if we take our eyes away it will crawl into some hidden spot and we will have to burn the house down to fix the problem.

"Let's just smash him with a book."

My mom shakes her head.

I roll my eyes. "Why not?"

"I am not killing creatures any more," she says.

I know why. I know all about ahimsa. But right now it seems impractical, foolish, and ridiculous.

"Mom, honestly, this spider could harm us. Like, how do you know it's not poisonous? I read it's hard to tell whether a spider is a black widow or a brown recluse."

My mother shudders and clenches her jaw tightly. "Where is that jar?" she screams. "Sasha, go get your sister. Now!"

I am not confident that my mother has this under control, so before I head downstairs I give some parting instructions. "Do not take your eyes off him." I am sure the spider is male. I know nothing about arachnids, but I am sure a female spider would not be cruel enough to terrorize a group of women living alone while the man of the house and resident spider killer is in Germany for three weeks.

I run down the stairs, skipping the whole last flight to jump straight to the bottom. The thick carpet cushions my fall, and I run into the kitchen. My sister is balanced on the counter, trying to get into the cabinet above the refrigerator. I am sure there are no jars in there, if we even have any in the house. "Just get a glass," I tell her, reaching up to catch her. We grab a thick clear glass and run upstairs to my mother.

"What the hell took you so long?" she demands. Her hands are shaking. The spider has moved and is now crawling slowly across the white wall toward my dad's study, as if it owns the place. Soon it might because all three of us are frozen. My sister starts to cry. My mother keeps her gaze fixed on the spider but gives my sister a shove. "Go to your room. I don't want you to see this."

Mariel doesn't budge. I hand my mom the glass and she shoves it back at me. "You do it." We are running out of time. If we pause another few seconds, the spider will make it into my dad's study, and who knows where to from there. I lunge at the wall with the glass and miss. The spider leaps from the wall, and I swear it's part cricket. It lands on my mother's shoulder, and she starts swatting and screaming. My sister is crying, and I am lunging. I hit my mother's shoulder and knock her to the ground.

The spider is on the move. It's traversing the woven carpet one nubby bump at a time, and I know if it gets to my sister's room, she's going to be sleeping in the second bed in my room until she's twenty. I can't let that happen.

"No-o-o!" I scream and take a flying leap. The glass lands half on the spider and half off. The spider twitches and hisses—for real, a spider hiss. That's what they do under stress. I gag and scream, but I hold the jar in place. I wiggle it a little and secure this prison to keep the wounded spider from moving anymore. I definitely crushed one of its legs. It's twitching, I am gagging, and my mother is handing me a roll of duct tape. I have no idea where she got this or how much time has passed. I am pressing the glass down with my full weight, sure that this spider will find its way out from under if I do not continue to hold the jar down with great commitment.

We start taping. We use almost the entire roll, securing the sticky gray tape all around the rim of the jar, then up and over the overturned jar. We affix the tape to the walls and make a big circle on the carpet. We cover the glass with so much tape that there is only one small "window" through which we can see the spider. It's still moving, but much slower.

"What about air holes?" Mariel says.

I look at Mom.

"He doesn't need them," she says. "Let's go to your room and play with Legos." They go to Mariel's room, leaving me alone with the spider.

The glass sits in the center of our hallway, right between my sister's room and my dad's study. I wonder how long the air in the taped-down glass will last. There is no food, but the spider will run out of air first. An hour, maybe two? I look and see that the spider is still. Maybe it has run out of air already.

When my father comes home, the jar is still there. I don't watch him remove it. I don't ask if the spider is dead. I know. We laugh about the story later. "Remember when mom was so afraid of a spider she put a glass on top and left it for two weeks?" It is funny and strange, and so is my mom. But is it *ahimsa*? I will never know how long it took for the spider to die. It was a fighter. But it might have been kinder to just smash it with a book.

Scattering the Ashes, Eventually

It's been a year, and we still haven't scattered my mother's ashes. I can't bear to part with them, and my father is in no hurry, either. We've been to Kripalu. We've seen the tree. It's small and looks a little sickly, but it's there. "I think we need to wait to make sure the tree makes it through the winter," my dad says in October.

The next month Gurudev is accused of sexual misconduct. Celibacy has been a major aspect of the ashram's appeal. Sex outside marriage was strictly forbidden among the disciples, and Gurudev claimed to have been celibate since 1968. The truth was more complicated. At least three of his female disciples admitted to having sex with him. At least one claimed it was coercion, with him promising her spiritual absolution if she slept with him. So it goes.

"I always knew he was a sleazebag," my Uncle Chris (Mary's spouse) tells us when we are in Cleveland for Christmas. "You could just tell. Those beady eyes. Those smarmy hands." His wife nods her head. My aunt hated Gurudev, too. She'd hated everything about my mother's spiritual path. Sometime later she tells me that she believes my mother is in hell. "I'd like to think otherwise," she says, "but I just think she was on the wrong path."

I cling to her words because I am stupid and twenty and because she looks like my mother and is closest in age. I wish I'd said, "Are you out of your mind saying that to a vulnerable twenty-year-old girl? How dare you?" Forty-year-old me defends that vulnerable young girl, but twenty-year-old me says nothing because I believe my aunt. My mother is lost and maybe in hell.

The powder, dirt, and bits of bone are sitting in a plastic bag inside an urn in our living room, and no one knows what to do. "We can't scatter them there now," my father says. He is kind of gleeful because as soon as he saw that reserved parking spot he knew that Gurudev was up to no good. "Those guys always turn out to be sleazebags, Sasha. Every time."

He's right. Bikram, founder of Bikram Yoga who will go down in a massive scandal. Anusara's founder, John Friend, who will have his own sex scandal. Amrit Desai. They are all sleazebags. As I delve deeper into the practice and meet more of the big-name male teachers, I will remember what my father says. They always turn out to be sleazebags. Is it yoga, or is it men? Maybe it's both.

The future of the ashram is unclear at the time. Kripalu immediately changes its name and severs any ties to Desai, but the wound is still bleeding. It's fresh and new, and no one knows how the scar tissue will form and what will remain of the spiritual center. The ashes sit on the mantel in our new house in Lexington, Massachusetts, where life continues to change and shift and morph around them.

We finally scatter the ashes in 2001. They've been moved from the mantel to a set of shelves over the kitchen table. We are finally ready to let them go. It's been eight years. I've gone to college and graduated. I've been engaged. I've ended it. I've fallen in love again. I've moved out of the house. It's time.

We choose Walden Pond because it's near my family's house, which is, ironically, in Belmont, Massachusetts, the town where Maggie, from Kripalu, lived. I look for her sometimes when I am walking around the neighborhood. I know it's unlikely I will run into her, and I might not even recognize her if I did, but I imagine that if I saw her I'd be happy to see someone here who was a witness.

I had a mom once. She was pretty special.

We pull the bag from the urn and stare at it in the center of our kitchen table. It's amazing what remains of a body: teeth, skin, fingernails, eyes, organs. They all burn down to such a small package. It's so simple, really. We spend our whole lives wishing we could be smaller. We diet. We push our bodies into spinning classes and run on treadmills. We hone and polish the body as though it were everything. We paint our nails and comb our hair. We dye the gray and wax the legs. We make love with our bodies and push ourselves into one another in so many ways. We touch. We hug. We sweat. We breathe.

When it's all over, everything fits into this little bag of gray powder with chunky bits of sand and gravel that look almost like nothing.

The body is so secondary. I can hear my mother whisper in my ear, and I know it to be true. Even though I will later regret the decision to scatter her ashes at Walden Pond and wish we'd chosen Kripalu instead, I know she will be at Kripalu no matter where she's scattered.

She will be in the wind. She will be in the changing leaves. She will be in the soft grass underfoot and the geese flying overhead. She will be in the trees, even though the plaque will disappear and we will never remember which one was hers. She will be all of them and none of them, and every bench, annex, and brick.

When I am there, I will feel her more than at any other place on Earth. So it really doesn't matter where we leave this dust.

Happy Baby
(The Pose You Hate)

Yoga teachers often say that the poses we hate teach us more than the ones we love. That may be true. My friend Julie is a yoga teacher with incredibly flexible hamstrings and strong arms. She can do splits easily and does a beautiful handstand and forearm stand. Her Crane pose—straight arms, knees pulled in tight, neck long and proud—is a thing of beauty. But she hates back bends.

We take a workshop together at the Yoga Journal Conference, an all-day practice with Baron Baptiste. As we close the first half of the day, he coaxes us into twelve Urdhva Dhanurasanas: upward bows; wheels; hands by ears, wrists toward the back of the room, fingers toward the front, knees pulling in toward midline, toes straight ahead, with straight arms and legs.

"The day we did eleven wheels too many," Julie jokes after class. She hates it because her spine isn't as flexible as the rest of her. It's humbling. It gets in the way of the feel-good portion of practice, the part where she feels accomplished. But as a teacher she knows otherwise.

"I have to practice that pose more than any other." She's right. The poses that humble us or challenge us often teach us the most.

I have hated different poses at different times in my life. When I was young, I hated the lotus position, largely because pulling my feet in toward my hip flexors is anatomically impossible for me. My hips just don't roll like that. They aren't open enough. My knees are not supple enough. To this day I still can't get into that position. I can do each leg separately, but never both at the same time.

But I've moved on from hating it. When the teacher cues lotus, I just prop my hips on a blanket and sit cross-legged. Although it limits some things—such as pressing into my palms and lifting my knees into my chest from lotus, or headstands with my legs in lotus—it doesn't ever make me feel inadequate. I have accepted this limitation.

When I go into yoga training, the two poses I hate most are Ananda Balasana (happy baby) and Utkatasana (chair). I hate chair because my body never feels quite right in the pose, with my weight on my heels, my hips back far enough that I can still see my toes, my arms up, an arch in my spine, a high gaze, and my palms reaching to touch overhead. This makes no sense in my body. I feel pulled and stretched and strained—and for what? I have no idea what this pose is strengthening or how it's helping my body.

There are few classes in a modern vinyasa practice that will not include Utkatasana. It's a key part of the ashtanga primary series, and modern vinyasa is an offshoot of those poses. I know Utkatasana is my lesson, so I dig in. I hold it longer than anyone in the class. I focus on the roots beneath me, my heels digging into the ground and the ground rising back up to meet me and support me. I feel my calves engage, and my thighs start to tremble and quake. I sit back another inch and breathe. I pull my knees in toward each other and sit back even deeper. I pull my belly in and engage my *bandhas*, pulling up on the pelvic floor and my lower belly. It's that inner fire and strength that keeps me lifted.

"You are stronger than you think you are," I always tell my students. "You always have more to give, more to push, and more to grow."

So it is with me, too. My palms may never touch over my head in a perfect Anjali Mudra. But I hate the pose a little less through exploring it, by forcing my body into the challenge and breathing through it. I also get stronger in the pose.

For weeks every breath is a question: How much longer are we here? How much longer do I hold? When can I fold? Then it changes. I explore the pose. Can I get edgier in my body? Can I step outside the comfort zone? Can I use each inhalation and exhalation to be present? Inhale here. Exhale now.

By the end of my first 200 hours, Utkatasana has gone from my most hated pose to my favorite. I hold my students in the pose now, sometimes for minutes at a time. I ask them to breathe and find the center. I tell them it's normal to project, to hate the pose and the class and the teacher. But all of it is about them. The posture we hate the most has the power to teach us more than any other.

Ananda Balasana is different. The pose is really just *malasana*, or squatting, while lying on one's back. The knees come in toward the armpits, and the hands reach for the outside edges of the feet. From the teacher's vantage point, sitting or standing at the head of a room, the pose is amusing. Thirty adults have their legs up in the air, open wide, and their butts prone. But the pose is a favorite for most people. They rock left to right and sigh. In many practices, the pose is the final one before Savasana, or corpse pose, the final rest.

No one hates the happy baby pose except me. I tell myself that I hate it because my hips are tight, and that is humbling for a little while. I am plagued by an old injury to my lower back when I lifted something heavy and spent the next year in pain. Sometimes when I am in happy baby pose I feel that strain again, but it's more than that. After a month of daily practice, the posture feels easy in my body. But I still hate it.

"How can anyone hate happy baby?" a friend teases me when we are on a yoga retreat in Mexico. "It's just like being a baby on your back in a crib. Toes up. Mommy peering down. It's such a safe and comforting pose."

It occurs to me that the same memories comforting her are breaking my heart. My mother's face, with her high cheekbones and rounded chin and the perfectly straight teeth that never required braces.

My father tells me that when I was a baby she sang "You Light Up My Life" by Debbie Boone to me every day, as I wriggled, squirmed, cooed, and kicked. "She loved you so much," he reminds me. "It brought tears to my eyes to watch."

I cue the happy baby pose in almost every class as a closing. The pose I hate so much is a favorite of many students. When a teacher offers students the option to include a pose that will make their practice feel complete just before final rest, nine out of ten students choose happy baby. I simply cut out the choice and offer the pose in almost every class.

"Make sure you feel happy in this pose," I tell my students. "Like a carefree baby." I say this nearly every time I call the pose. Physically, the pose isn't a problem for me anymore, but I cry every time I do it, anyway.

Another Tarot Card Reading

One of the best things about living in northern New Jersey is that you can find anything in the world. The proximity to New York City means that a lot of people are used to getting sushi, vegan food, and Ethiopian food all on the same day. It's easy for me to find somewhere Samara and I can learn to read tarot cards together.

I uncovered my mother's tarot deck in a box of old letters. The Mother of Peace deck is round and is considered a "feminist deck." Every picture is a woman: bathing, wearing a cat suit, decorated in war paint. Each picture comes from a goddess or a female warrior. It is beautiful, and I haven't seen it in years. I didn't even know I had it.

I look to the universe for signs. I am two years into teaching yoga. This is a sign.

Samara and I pull into a parking lot in Montclair, New Jersey, on a frigid February morning to go to the Montclair Metaphysical Center. It doesn't look like a place to meet psychics and mediums. The carpet is gray and dusty. The waiting room is small and cramped. The walls are lined with ointments and potions, crystals and tumbled rocks, all for sale. Samara immediately wants all the purple ones.

"After," I tell her, pulling her into the room where our class is being held. We are late. We each have our own deck, the very basic, traditional, Rider-Waite deck.

A tarot deck is a lot like a deck of playing cards. There are four suits—cups, swords, wands, and pentacles—of fourteen cards each, called the Minor Arcana. There are another twenty-two cards called the Major Arcana. These are what you might call the high-drama cards; they have names like the Priestess, the Lovers, the Tower, and Death.

Most who are new to tarot take some of the cards too literally—for instance, thinking that the Death card means death. But in tarot that's not how it works. The Death card can mean transformation, deep change, a new beginning, or a need to let go of something that is dragging you down. The Lovers card doesn't necessarily indicate a new love. It could mean any strong relationship with a pull and chemistry, such as a business partnership or a friendship. It can also refer to a polarity within yourself and indicate that there is a choice to be made.

A tarot reading is very subjective. The reader uses intuition, relying in part on how a card makes him or her feel. Samara and I charge our decks with crystals and sleep with them overnight to infuse them with our energy. There is no book that can fully tell us what each card means or how we should interpret it. Once you've familiarized yourself with the deck, the real power comes from within you. The tarot deck serves as a tool of your intuition and energy; it is not just some parlor game to predict the future.

"Trust what the cards tell you," our teacher says.

She's short and soft, her body open and inviting. Her hair is curly and tight, and when she talks her voice is soothing and melodic, almost hypnotic. "This is all about your intuition. Not what I tell you. Close your eyes. Shuffle."

I close my eyes and shuffle, and as I do I feel the cards move through my fingers until my fingertips vibrate with the energy. I can see it now. It's like what I tell my students: Honor the body you have. Show up for it. It will show you how to move.

I draw the Magician. I shuffle again and draw the same card. I draw other cards, too, but I keep coming back to this card again and again, four times.

The card is yellow, with a man standing in the center. An infinity symbol is above his head, like a lit halo. He wears a red robe and there is a table in front of him. On the table is a cup, a sword, a pentacle, and a wand. He holds a crystal in his right hand and all around him is a light. There are white and red vines and flowers around the edge of the card. He is pointing down with his left hand.

"What does it mean?" I ask, because I don't know.

"Only you can say, sweetie."

"But isn't there like an obvious meaning, something you can explain? Just to get me started?"

She smiles at me. I know the answer. Only I can tell. It's the light I keep seeing. It's an aura of sorts. All the light seems to stem from the crystal in the Magician's right hand, but the light seems bigger than that, as if it comes from the soul. The Magician makes things grow. The energy that comes from him helps to bring life and move all the suits and bring them to the table.

The Magician is riding his own magic and intuition.

"Does that mean something to you?"

My own magic, my own energy, my own path—yes, it means something to me.

For Samara, it's more intuitive. She is nervous at first, especially when the teacher asks us to rotate and read for people we don't know. But she is open, too. "I think this means change is on the way," she says, first cautiously and then more enthusiastically as she sees the impact. The woman she's reading for is enthralled. She fully believes.

Later I ask Samara what she thought.

"It was cool," she says. "I want to keep my cards under my pillow."

She knows already what it took me thirty years to learn.

Reiki Attunement and Seeing Energy

It's been decades since I believed I could see energy. I haven't tried since the day I saw Mrs. Vaughn's aura, the red light shooting from her hips and the blue all around her. It's like I put it all in a box, wrapped it up, and forgot it. But this level-one Reiki attunement is bringing it back.

It's a full-day session in a yoga studio. The room is large and dark, and the energy is always strong. I teach five classes a week and have seen more prana dripped on this floor than I can even say. I've slipped on it. I've nearly broken my tailbone, thanks to the prana. But the room isn't heated today. There are six of us, and we are all yoga teachers.

"Light workers." Carol Anne, my Reiki teacher, calls us that, but are we?

I struggle with the light. Yoga is getting me there, but I am a cynic, the first to feel a white flash of anger when something is wrong, unfair, or unjust. My mother used to say that my wires were crossed, that the piece of me that felt love was crossed with the piece of me that feels

anger, so when something feels unjust or wrong, I lash out. I scream.
I thrash. I make enemies. I say things I don't mean, and it makes it
hard for people to see my softness.

"I thought you hated me when I first met you," one of my fellow
yoga teachers tells me.

She isn't the first one. I've been called intimidating, aloof, guarded,
and snappy. I get claustrophobic in hugs I don't initiate. I'm incredibly
sensitive about other people's desire to be touched. Ashley, my friend
and the manager of the biggest studio I teach in, always tells me to
touch people more, to give them assistance.

Most people like to be touched, but I don't. At least, I don't
before the yoga takes over. I used to cringe in class when the teacher
approached me, and I would try to will her to walk away from me.
Please don't press on my back during the Child pose. Please don't rub
my forehead in Savasana. But I've changed. Now I like the assistance.
When I see the teacher, I drop to my knees and sink my hips back on
my heels. Touch me! Touch me!

But even as I grow more comfortable with being touched, I still
shy away from doing the touching. What if I inadvertently trigger
trauma? What if I transfer bad energy?

Reiki is energy work that sometimes uses the power of touch. It
can also be performed from a distance, but it often involves touch.
It is a transfer, a movement of blocked energy, a way of clearing out
anything that is stopped up or at an impasse so that a healthy flow can
happen throughout the body. Everyone in the class considers him- or
herself a light worker—everyone but me. I want to be, but I'm not yet.

We meditate. We close our eyes. We wait for the teacher to choose
us from the circle, and when she does choose me, she leads me to a
chair and seats me. My eyes are closed. I feel something, but I don't

know what. The energy crackles and shifts. Then she blows on my head, and I feel warm from head to toe. She walks me back to the circle, and I sit down again.

What just happened?

We break into two groups of three, since there are two massage tables, and start working on each other. The women in my group, Ashley and Ashley (an odd coincidence given it's my father's name as well). I know well. I am comfortable, so I place my hands on Ashley and start to move them. Reiki can be performed at a distance or without touching a person. But in this case, I feel called to be hands-on. My hands feel warm and tingly, almost achy. I find a spot and stay there. Is something happening? I open one eye, then the other.

Carol tells us we have to feel. Each of us will experience the energy differently. Some of us will work with our eyes closed. Others will prefer to have their eyes open. I am a seer. I know this instinctively. As soon as I open my eyes I see streaks of blue all around Ashley's body. I see the blocks. I know where the energy needs to move to. I see where her chakras are out of line. The blue is dancing, flickering, moving all around her body. I giggle. A couple of people look at me. It's magic, like fairies dancing on her. Does anyone else see this? Am I going crazy?

When the other Ashley gets on the table, it shuts down. I see nothing.

"You have to have faith in it," Carol Anne tells us later. "You have to believe. You will grow stronger with it if you practice."

I think back to the night with my mother when I had seen auras. I am sure I stopped it then because I was scared. How could this be real? How could this energy be so present and yet so unseen? But the truth is that we miss things all the time.

Rob is a scientist, a practical person in almost every way. One of his favorite topics is string theory, the idea that much of what we know in the world is made up of tiny vibrating "strings" and that they make up the entire universe. But we can't see them, and it's not proven. I struggle to understand this. It's where our life views meet, because according to string theory, there are multiple dimensions and things happening all the time that we simply cannot see with the naked eye. There are whole worlds and dimensions that may be undetected by us because we simply are not equipped to see them. It explains everything, from ghost sightings to aliens to what people see when they take ayahuasca in the Peruvian jungle. It explains the blue I see, too—or at least it does for Rob.

"I believe it," he tells me, when I describe the wispy dancing energy.

He feels it later, too, when I clean his chakras and give him a Reiki healing. I am not a light worker yet, but I am getting there, inching closer every time I open my eyes and mind to something I'd previously dismissed.

"There is so much out there we just don't know," Rob tells me.

He means this in a scientific way, like space travel and discovering the bottom of the sea, like theories of physics not yet proven.

I agree. There's a lot to know and learn, and there are lots of ways we still have to grow.

Mayan Sound Healing

My friend Julie and I enter the sound healing space in single file. Each woman on this yoga retreat in Tulum, Mexico, is blessed with some ashes and a light touch to the third-eye chakra, the space between the eyebrows. Three women in white robes greet us. My greeter has wavy blond hair falling to her hips, with a crown of flowers. She looks like an ad for the clothing retailer Anthropologie.

We are invited into the circle to get comfortable on one of the mats that surround an open space in the center. I see skin drums and some kind of wooden xylophone, as well as two large crystal bowls. The only man in the room sits in the center, legs folded in the lotus position, and just like the women, he has hair down to his waist, streaked with gray; his beard is equally long and gray. His eyes are closed, and his hands are palms down on his knees.

My friend nudges my arm. "Sister wives," she mouths, and I giggle until I am quickly silenced by stern looks from the three women at the front of the room.

Once I settle on my mat, I realize how dark it is. It's well after nine o'clock at night, so the only illumination comes from candles placed in each corner of the yoga *shala* (Sanskrit word that means "house"). We are so close to the ocean that we can hear the waves rolling in and out, but there is no other sound in the room once I am on my mat, except the floor creaking as others find their spots. The whole space smells of the sage burning in three different locations.

No talking.

As soon as we are settled, the Mayan sound healing begins. At first it is just chanting; then the drums are added. Someone plays the bowls, and I am drifting, floating, moving from sound to sound, losing track of the day and time and even my body. Have we been here an hour? Two hours? Less? The sound and vibrations and the breeze are conspiring to pull me away. I imagine myself hopping from one musical note to another, like some kind of Nintendo game in my head.

I become aware of someone standing over me. I can feel her fanning something over my body; then, even though she never touches me, I jerk to the side, feeling as if she's just reached into me and pulled something out, as though I am an avocado and she's taken the pit.

Is this good or bad? I don't know. I am floating on something: a memory, my mother's perfume, the lotion she wore at the very end. Victoria's Secret's fragrance line. The scent of raspberry she admired on her hospice nurse so much that we bought her a set for her last birthday, November 1, seventeen days before she died.

There are two smells I once couldn't tolerate: raspberry glace and lilies—the latter because everyone sent lilies after my mother died. I smell them now, here in this room, along with the incense and the musk and the patchouli each woman wears on her neck. Here I am okay. These memories feel safe, as though I can steep myself in them without getting burned.

Later, as we leave the circle, I have no idea how long I have been there. We file out to the beach, none of us speaking. We look up at the stars, and I watch the brightest one. It's so far away, yet at some point, in some distant time, I know my mother looked up at the same sky. She saw the same stars. It's all so much bigger than I could have imagined.

These smells don't make me sick any more. My practice pulls me ever closer to her. So many decades have passed, yet this star reminds me, in universal terms, that it's all a blink.

First Mammogram: A Legacy of Cancer

The machine is not what I expect. My vision of my first mammogram has been clouded by bad movies and articles on the Internet. I imagine someone out of a Roald Dahl novel, a woman with a long nose (there'd have to be warts), a long black skirt, and at least four long fingernails poking at my breast and smashing it into one of the machines I'd seen on my tour through Europe's many torture museums. I imagined rusty anvils and pointy prods still covered in the blood of the last woman subjected to this procedure.

Obviously, getting a mammogram is nothing like this. Aside from my fear that I will be strapped into a medieval torture device, the whole experience is not what I expected. I'd spent twenty-five years dreading something that, it turns out, is nothing like that at all.

Here in this breast center in a giant hospital in Montclair, New Jersey, I am far away from my mother, both physically and spiritually. But the actual process of creating X-rays of my breasts for the radiologist to examine and use as a baseline for all my future mammograms is relatively uneventful.

I had put it off for months—years. When I turned thirty I was tested for the BRCA genes that cause so many of the most deadly forms of ovarian and breast cancer. The test came back negative, but with a mother, a maternal grandmother, and a maternal aunt with the disease, I have a genetic link. "Negative" only means unknown genetic status. I am still on a high-risk protocol.

There are cute accessories in the waiting room, pamphlets detailing different kinds of lumps and how to find them. Maybe that's not cute at all, but it's reading material.

I am led into a dressing room to change into my soft fluffy robe, which is much nicer than a stained hospital gown. The cream-colored room has soft lighting and a full-length mirror. I am convinced it must be concave, because honestly, I look pretty good if I choose to believe it.

The room has a basket, too, like the kind you'd find in a spa. I half expect it to be full of cherry blossom–scented lotions and heart-shaped soaps. But it isn't. It's full of wet wipes under a sign: Make sure you have removed all deodorant and body lotions before stepping into the exam room.

I sniff my armpits, which reminds me that yogi deodorant is missing all the key ingredients that make deodorant actually work. Therefore I stink. I use a wipe under both arms. I open another packet and swipe again. I am going to get up close and personal with a Roald Dahl character. The least I can do is smell nice for her.

Then I am done stalling, and I need to open the door. Each time I step into a hospital room of any kind, it brings it all back. I do what I have to do.

Instead of the expected rusty anvils and Roald Dahl villain, or at least a man in a butcher's apron, a nice woman in her early sixties greets me, with gray hair falling to her shoulders, and soft warm hands. This is an important detail when someone is feeling you up. She is wearing a dainty gold cross around her neck, and her voice is smooth and reassuring.

"My daughter gets her mammograms here, too," she tells me. "This is not the way mothers and daughters usually behave."

We both laugh. They must be close. I wonder if her daughter looks like her mother. Do they share the same turned-up nose and rosy cheeks?

I used to cry when I saw mothers and daughters at the mall. They'd be laughing and shopping, and I'd be secretly wishing one of them would fall into a hole and sprain her ankle—not a break, just a sprain, enough to make them stop smiling, laughing, and bonding.

I am over that now, maybe because I have my own daughters. I can smile at the thought of a mother handling her adult daughter's breasts and the awkwardness that might create. But it wouldn't only be awkward. It would also be comforting, like a living room breast exam. Not quite so medieval.

I channel this woman's daughter. I imagine living in a family in which there is no history of breast cancer and the only experience I have with the disease is from my mother, a nurse who spends all day seeing women exposed and vulnerable. She puts them at ease with her jokes, and I am especially relaxed because she is my mom. She changed my diapers. She and I fought over my prom dress. No one knows me better. If I am her daughter, I am also not scared that they will find a lump. I assume all will be fine, as it always has been for my mother.

But this nurse is not my mother. My hands shake, and I am suddenly cold. This reaction is not new. She applies round white stickers with metal dots on the tip of each nipple. I look like some kind of space-age burlesque queen; they are clearly made for women with large breasts, and my 34DD cups spilleth over. The pasties are barely enough to cover the tip of one nipple.

"What are these?" I ask. "Just decoration?"

She laughs. "This just differentiates between the nipple and the breast."

I am grateful that she is warm and funny and seems to be interested in making this traumatic event far less so.

"Just take one shoulder out," she says, and puts my breast on a plastic tray.

I wish my husband were here to see this. It seems so absurd. She starts to lower the machine, flattening my breast against the tray. When I am uncomfortable, she lowers it a millimeter more.

"Sorry," she says, puckering her face as if she's had a lemon. "Is that terribly uncomfortable?"

It isn't. I tell her. She snaps the photos and releases my breast, and then we have to do the same thing on the other side. The whole process takes maybe ten minutes instead of the hours I'd imagined enduring the mean old schoolmarm and the anvils.

I am still uneasy. I am not sure how I will sleep tonight, knowing that these films have been made. I imagine calcifications, percentages and grades, and estrogen-positive versus estrogen-negative. All these words mean little to me, but I know they are the language of cancer, and I am scared. I think of my mother and what the cancer did to her body.

I am thirty-eight years old, still three years younger than she was when she found the lump. But I notice more and more changes lately that make me think of my mom: the way my veins pop in my hands, the softness of my neck, the wrinkling of the skin on my chest, and the fine lines forming around my eyes.

When I was sixteen, forty-five seemed so old. I thought then that she had lived a long(ish) life already. But it was still short, still too painfully, horrifically, tragically brief. But it wasn't so young that she hadn't done anything. She'd trekked through the Andes and back-packed twice through Europe on five dollars a day.

Now, at thirty-eight, with forty-five looming just ahead for me, it seemed different. I just finished nursing my youngest child. My oldest is learning fractions. They are practically still fetal. They need me in tip-top form.

The next twelve hours, waiting for the images to be reviewed, will be rough.

Going Vegan

The guinea pigs make me go vegan. Rob and I are in Peru on a weeklong trip to Machu Picchu. Along the most famous Incan trail and the Sacred Valley, our guide introduces us to the Incan way of life. We see hundreds of species of corn and farming techniques that exceeded anything we think they should have known. I feel a spirituality that closely mirrors the one I am discovering through yoga. Pachamama is the Incan fertility goddess who rules planting and harvesting and who lives in the curve of the mountains.

Back home, Donald Trump has been elected president of the United States. He wins despite the rampant misogyny in his campaign, the multiple allegations of sexual assault against him, and his "grab them by the pussy" bragging on a previous radio show. The words ring in my ears. Pussy. Yoni, the divine feminine.

How much have we lost? How far have we deviated from all that is beautiful, life-affirming, and meaningful in this world?

Peru wakes me up. There were others like me once upon a time, and others like my mother. I am having a spiritual orgasm. I make

Rob stop at every shaman store. I buy packets of herbs and rolled stones. One is for creativity, another for prosperity, and another for the health and good fortune of our children.

The Incans worship the earth. Three animals feature heavily in every piece of art, stonework, and weaving: the condor, which represents the sky, soaring high and proud; the puma, which stalks the earth and represents all our material desires and Earthly wisdom; and the snake, which represents the underground, all we cannot see, which supports us without us knowing.

We visit the temple of Pachamama and learn that the moon cycles of women were revered, that there was an appreciation for the feminine and for all things divine and womanly.

But they also slaughter guinea pigs by the thousands. *Cuy*, or guinea pig meat, is a delicacy throughout the Andes that many in Peru, Ecuador, and Bolivia eat for special celebrations such as birthdays. Guinea pigs are everywhere. We see them as sweet stuffed animals for tourists to buy in the public markets, all dressed up in traditional Andean clothing or made of the softest alpaca fur. We see some real guinea pigs in restaurants, where they run around and wrinkle their noses, squeaking at people to feed them, touch them, and play. Their images are on billboards and restaurant signs.

Two months ago we had a guinea pig birth in my house. A few months after we tragically lost one of my daughter's guinea pigs, we got a second guinea pig at an all-female pet store. Samara was thrilled when we brought home her new little friend. She named her Black Widow. But "she" was not a female. We found this out early in the spring.

"Lila looks fat," Rob told me one morning, referring to our original pet. He forgot that my father ran an accidental guinea pig–breeding operation in my childhood. He forgot that I would know right away what was going on.

"She's pregnant." It was obvious once I pointed it out. Her little white sides were bulging with babies. We stared. The babies moved. We placed our hands on her belly as they kicked and moved and punched. Lila's little legs struggled to move under all the extra weight, so she mostly stayed still.

We packed a box full of cotton and took her to the vet. "I'd say four or five babies," the vet reported. "Maybe in a week or two."

I couldn't stop watching Lila. I brought her carrots while I was working downstairs. I posted photos of her on Facebook. I had never felt such compassion for another living creature. I remembered that discomfort: the swollen ankles, the inability to move in bed, the jabs to the ribs, and then the labor.

I Googled. It was too much. I read about guinea pig deaths and half-born piglets, and I called the vet. "What do I do if she is in distress?"

"You call us."

"In the middle of the night?" No one seemed to grasp what this meant to me. I needed Lila to be safe. I needed her to make it. I spent hours by her cage, my computer in hand. Is this it? She waddled to the water bottle and then collapsed beneath it. No babies. We waited.

We took Black Widow out of the cage and made him a new one. I wanted to love him still. It wasn't his fault he had a surprise penis. Is that what nature is? Grab them by the pussy? First Lila watched her sister die next to her, and now this from her new "sister."

I was wracked with guilt, both the rational and the irrational kind. I thought if I could make her live, if I could deliver these babies safely into the world, maybe I could undo some of the damage this president was doing. It was irrational and crazy. It wasn't about the guinea pigs.

But it was. I could not let Lila die. I had promised Samara. So I stayed up late to be by her side. I napped by the cage in the middle of the day. We had no way of knowing when labor would start, but I wanted to be there if there was trouble.

Maybe all of this was my penance. As a child I had been too rough with my guinea pigs, Karen and Brian. I threw them in the air. I didn't always catch them. Karen had a bloody nose once. Brian's teeth once bled. I remembered that I had done that to them. I felt the heat crawling into my face. If I could deliver these babies safely and make sure they lived, I could make peace with Karen and Brian and apologize.

Five days later the babies appeared. I missed the whole thing. I went to sleep one night, and by five o'clock the next morning four babies were nestled by their mama. I had done the research. I knew that guinea pig babies were born fully formed, not hairless, like mice or rats, and not helpless, like human babies. Even so it was a shock. Four tiny souls, perfectly formed miniature guinea pigs, no bigger than the span of my daughter's tiny palm. Their noses twitched, they squeaked, and they drank milk from their mama.

Lila looked dazed, but she ate the placentas and cleaned up as though it had never happened. I gave her carrots by the dozen and watched her eat them. The babies pushed and jumped over each other to get to her nipples. They crawled underneath her and squeaked and somersaulted.

Later we kept the female baby and found new homes for the males, except Black Widow, who had his own cage far from the females.

So there are three guinea pigs back home in the States while we are in Peru. We are paying someone to lovingly care for them daily—to hold them and pet them in addition to giving them food and water.

When people come around with hairless carcasses of *cuy*, the skin thick and pink but obviously still fully formed guinea pigs, I feel the bile start to rise. I want to be culturally sensitive. I am a traveler and a lover of other cultures. This is a delicacy.

We drive through one town where every other restaurant serves *cuy*. It's not enough to simply have it on the menu. Men stand outside in chef hats, holding the burnt carcasses on sticks.

"*Cuy! Cuy! Cuy!*" they call.

Giant guinea pigs made of plastic and wearing chef hats stand outside some of the restaurants, their paws on their bellies. "Eat me! Eat me!"

I cannot.

"It's like a guinea pig Holocaust in this town," Rob says.

I laugh, but it isn't funny.

That night we are offered alpaca as part of our dinner. It's in a stew and well disguised. I choke it down to be polite, but I feel sick later. It's the last meat I will ever eat. When I come home, I commit to vegetarianism, and within a month I give up dairy and eggs, too.

In my second 200-hour yoga training, we studied veganism. We were asked to focus on our eating habits and what they do to the planet. But we were never asked what they do to us. "I believe in the food chain," I said during one discussion. "I believe that we are at the top of it."

But when I stop eating meat, I feel more authentic in my commitment to *ahimsa*, to doing no harm. But something else happens, too. I connect. When I ate unconsciously, I shut down a piece of myself with every egg consumed. I denied my humanity with every turkey sandwich. By saying no to animal products, not only am I reaffirming my humanity, my empathy, and my commitment to *ahimsa*. I become part of the universal truth, the prana that flows through us all. I am not at the top of the food chain. I am no better than a cow, a chicken, or a goat—or a guinea pig.

It's like a light switch for me. One day I can eat meat. The next I can't. It's political, too. There is so much anger, toxicity, and cruelty in the world. If I can make one small change to my refrigerator and my plate and save one animal, why wouldn't I? If one less creature will die needlessly and heartlessly because of the choice I make as a consumer, how can I not make that choice?

"Are you going to be one of those annoying vegans who tells everyone about your life change?" Rob says.

I am. But it's not because I think I am better. It's because I believe we *all* are. We are better than these unconscious lives, better than the lies we tell ourselves every time we grill a rack of ribs.

My mother knew all this. She knew it when she slipped the tofu in the chili and when she forced us to eat sun burgers instead of cow burgers, tempeh instead of bacon, and avocado instead of butter. For my mother, it was about her health and Earth. For me, it is about the creatures, big and small, that we live with. It's all a philosophy of doing no harm, which is central to the yogic life. How did it take me nearly forty years to figure it out?

Ahimsa. I get it now. My training is complete.

Be here now, my mother would say. I am. And how.

9. Integrating

INTEGRATION.

SAVASANA

(CORPSE POSE, FINAL REST)

THIS IS THE MOST IMPORTANT PART OF CLASS,
WHEN EVERYTHING COMES TOGETHER IN SILENCE
AND STILLNESS.

OUR MOVEMENTS INTEGRATE INTO THE BODY.

Be Here Now: My First Teaching Job

My first job in yoga is at Shakti, the little studio down the street from my house. In Hinduism Shakti is the divine feminine, a goddess of fertility and creation. Shakti represents energy and all things powerful: momentum, movement. It is a perfect fit for embarking on my career—a new creation.

Anna, the teacher who owns the studio, walks as if she were floating. She embodies yoga, with her undyed hair, soft smile, and loose clothing. I imagine her in white Birkenstocks with massage bottoms. Her earth-colored ensembles remind me of my mother's clothes.

Anna has hundreds and hundreds of hours of training in ayurveda (the traditional medicine of India), massage, and different styles of yoga.

"Anna is the real deal," I am told when I announce my new job.

She also knows Kripalu well from training there. We bond over it, and she offers me a job right away—the six o'clock sunrise class, twice a week. I am ecstatic.

The space is beautiful. The front is small but packed with beautiful things. A golden cushion on top of a wooden chair is the only seating. Most of the space is for the retail sale of items such as old earrings with lacy filament, beaded necklaces, loose cotton clothing in bright colors, essential oils, music CDs, and mala beads. Shoes are taken off at the entrance. When a class is crowded, the shoes pile up on a tray. It's easy to see what's happening in the practice space, at the end of a long hallway, just by observing the number of shoes. As a teacher, payment depends on shoes: the more shoes, the better the payment.

The studio is bigger than it appears from outside. A long hallway lined with doors leads to the practice space. There are two rooms for massage and various healing techniques, as well as a bathroom. Small windows let in fresh air, aided by multiple ceiling fans. The whole space is painted a soft orange. It's a bright color, but it works.

My body feels stimulated just by walking in the door.

The first class I teach at Shakti—and my first for money any-where—is on a Friday morning in late April. My knees feel wobbly with nerves the whole way there. Will anyone show up? Will they like my music? Will I remember the flow? So far my teaching practice has consisted of testing cues on my children, the hour-long final exam class I taught, and my audition at Baker. This is the first public class I have ever taught for paying customers.

The studio is dark and quiet when I arrive, but Springfield Avenue is busy. Cars rush by and people hurry down the street, even before six o'clock. The studio stands between a pizza shop and a smoothie place, with its bright prayer flags and a large colorful sign. The avenue is full of restaurants, nail salons, braiding salons, and oil-change shops. On one end is the turn into Millburn, one of the richest towns in the United States. On the other end is East Orange, an urban area with a

fairly high crime rate. Shakti sits just between these two towns. The
street reflects this diversity. There are as many check-cashing places
as organic groceries and farmer's markets.

I arrive early and sit behind the desk, fighting the urge to squeal
like a child. I am behind the desk! I can check people in! I have a
mind-body log-in! I feel a bit the way I did when I was five and would
play grocery store with my friends. The thrill of being behind a desk,
able to handle cash and concerns, isn't lost on me, even though it's
been thirty years. My hands are shaking with glee and nerves.

One student arrives, and she turns out to be the only one. The
stereo doesn't work. It's full of static and unsteady. I turn off the music
and teach in silence. She's a beginner, so I model every pose. This is
Downward Dog. This is Chaturanga. It's slow and personal. I have to
modify and shift my plans according to what her body needs.

It's good practice. I keep thinking this, even as my classes stay the
same. Each day, just as I think no one will come, one person stumbles
in. It's never the same person. It goes on like this for weeks, twice a
week. It's late spring, so getting up at five in the morning isn't the
chore it will become in November.

Shakti's pay structure gives teachers a small percentage of whatever the student pays, so if the student uses a Groupon coupon, I
would get roughly three dollars for an hour of teaching. I keep telling myself that I am not in it for the money, that I make most of
my money from writing, and this is true. I also know I'm getting
great practice. But private yoga classes often run a hundred dollars
an hour; I am teaching them for three. I am also eager for the energy
of a group class.

I quit and apply elsewhere. I can walk to six yoga studios from
my house. I can practice kundalini, ashtanga, iyengar, vinyasa, hot

vinyasa, prenatal, yin, restorative, mommy and me, and several other self-branded styles of yoga.

Instagram is full of beautiful blond yoga instructors doing handstands. Every muscle in their bodies gleams. They wear perfect outfits from yoga-wear designers who vie for the opportunity to be featured at their professional galleries, perfectly matched in tone and color scheme, with the occasional sponsored post promoting jewelry companies, clothing designers, and shoes. It's overwhelming, and it's changing what yoga means.

My mother taught classes at the Jewish Community Center. She taught slow and mindful yoga to an older population that had probably received recommendations for it from their doctors. "Try yoga, it's this great form of mindfulness and stretching."

My mother loved introducing people to the practice, because back then it *was* an introduction. Now it is something else. Everyone practices yoga.

I audition at a new studio near me. One of the teachers from Baker Street, whose classes I loved on Saturday mornings, is a partner in the studio, and I am hopeful. The audition is round-robin style, and I am one of three teachers auditioning.

I turn on my music and set up my flow. I teach for twenty minutes, my hands shaking but my voice strong. I wait a few days, and they tell me thanks but no thanks. I ask for further explanation and am told that I am not likable enough, that people come back to teachers they connect with, and I am too aloof. I cry in the bathroom for a good half hour.

But I am determined. I audition at my gym, Lifetime. The yoga director is the impossibly gorgeous Ashley. She has long blond hair and a perfect face, with white teeth and perfect abs. She asks me to prepare two small sections of a class. Then we sit and talk. She's just injured her neck, and we chat about that. She asks me how many classes I am looking to teach.

"Five," I tell her. "At least."

She looks at me straight on, which is what I love about her. She stares into souls. "Wow. You really want to teach."

I feel the energy shift. I know she gets me. I forget the cruel rejection. I know this is home. She offers me an opportunity to take another 200-hour training through Lifetime, which I do with my discount as a yoga teacher. Lifetime has a specific style of yoga, which includes a free-flow portion in every class. Some people love it and some hate it. I learn to love it. Over the course of the three-month training, during which I really learn to teach, I grow close to each person. I learn to love Ashley and the two other Ashleys who are in the training program. They are both hired.

Our yoga is in a hot room. We collapse into heaps at the end of class, exhausted and drained, soaked and ecstatic. These women are some of the best I've ever known, trading secrets and tricks and Spotify playlists as though it's nothing.

There are no friends like yoga friends, no connections like the ones made in a yoga studio. I learn this quickly. These women are supportive and strong. So what if they are ten years younger than I am? That's beside the point.

By the end of my first year of teaching, my schedule is full, with two classes at Baker Street and five at Lifetime. I teach Mondays at 5:45 AM and then late into the evening at Lifetime.

The practice is different from anything I've done before. I have two yin classes. I learn to put out the fire we build in vinyasa. I've learned about so many different kinds of yoga and teachers. I feel at home when I walk into Baker and Lifetime. Every other studio was a bad fit. These are the only ones for me. It's like Kriplua was for my mother: home. I know this will grow and shift and change, too. It's the one truth on which we can rely.

I remember the jagged scar across my mother's chest where her breast had been. She never once told me it hurt or that she felt less feminine or concerned about her beauty, her femininity, and her sexuality. Was she? There are secrets you keep from a twelve-year-old, especially when she's your daughter. But the journals I read don't mention it, either. Was she scared? Sad? Worried about her marriage?

Every day I inch closer to her in age and body. Three children have changed my taut belly to something softer. It's not quite jelly, but it's no longer rippled, muscled, and flat. The silvery streaks on my lower belly aren't obvious or pronounced, but I see them every time I take off my shirt, like messages written with a Sharpie on a bathroom wall. *Samara was here, then Alan, then Adara.*

This body was their home, as my mother's was once for me. I moved and sloshed and kicked my feet into her ribs while she meditated and walked and did a thousand Cat or Cow poses. I can imagine her then, twenty-eight and strong, big with child and promise and youth, moving and imagining. What would the baby look like? Could we have imagined what would be? I imagine myself safe inside, while somewhere in her body other cells rebelled and plotted against her. Am I somehow to blame? Or is this the way it had to be?

We are so alike, my mother and I, and so different: her secrets and my truth. Her silence and my loud mouth. Her meditation and my vinyasa. We are forever linked.

As I get closer to the age she was when I last knew her, I am shifting. I take walks with no music. I feel my foot slide across the floor.

I am aware of every bristle on my toothbrush as it slides across my gums and the cool porcelain of the sink chilling my hip as it pushes against it, along with the pressure on my hand as I lean against it. I feel the soft beat and pulse of my blood as it moves and redistributes. My body is changing as I move out of my childbearing years. My period is shifting: the cycle shortening, the bleeding unpredictable. Some moons are short and light, some long and heavy. I don't try to predict it anymore. I just prepare.

Samara is approaching the corresponding change at the other end of the cycle, and my eyes tear up at the thought: a mother at the tail end of her reproductive years just as a daughter enters hers. The fourth generation of our family. Same story. Maybe this is how it is with mothers and daughters. We look back, we look forward, but do we ever really see each other? Do we ever really know the truth? She is mine and I am hers, and on and on through the generations, but in the end we belong only to ourselves. We shape, we mold, we create—ourselves.

The yoga my mother practiced was the yoga for her. The yoga I practice is the yoga for me. The more I learn about the practice and the more I move in my own body, the more I see this. I am aware of every shift. My runs have turned into walks. My handstand practices have turned into meditation.

The beauty in every moment is not lost on me anymore. I edge toward my mother every day. Someday, just a few years from now (God willing), I will be older than she ever got to be. I will cross the barrier I have been dreading since I was sixteen. What then? What's the script on forty-five? It will be entirely new, but it will be freeing, too.

In yoga we say *be here now*. But we also say there is no perfect yogi. We are all on the path, struggling toward enlightenment. We push. We fight. We scream obscenities in traffic. Samara and Alan call them

"Mommy's traffic words." They all rhyme with *truck*. It's comforting and painful to know this is a journey and never a destination.

We keep coming back to the breath every time we stumble and fall, every time we start making a to-do list in our heads and scatter our eyes around the room and our thoughts around the world. We return. We breathe—in, out, in, out.

I fear the future. I fear a lump in my breast and chemotherapy. I fear jagged scars where my full breasts used to be. I fear doctors and tests and ports and hair loss. But I fear not being here more than anything.

As daughters, our fates are intrinsically tied to our mothers' fates. It's our birthright. I watch Samara watching me. From me she learns to wash hands, tie shoes, and stomp feet when things go wrong. She mirrors back all my worst behavior, like entitlement: "If I don't like going to the gym, none of us should have to go." Her favorite band is touring on the West Coast, and she expects us to buy tickets and fly to San Diego on a whim to see a band she won't like in five years. I tell her this. She doesn't believe me. Of course she'll like them. She'll like them forever.

I marvel at the simplicity of her expectations and the selfishness. Reframed, it is something else: a belief in her own worth, in her right to exist and take up space with her desires. It's beautiful in its own way.

This dance is crazy, this changing of the guards. My age, her youth. My mother, the impossible ghost. I chase her through the halls of my mind, wondering. What would she think of this decision? This class? This dinner? Would she text me her thoughts on the Bhagavad Gita as we read it together? Would she take my classes? Would she think they were too physical, too *focused on the poses*?

Where's the real yoga? Would she wonder that?

I am inspired by the past and by my mother, by what she taught me and what it took me decades to learn. I am inspired by the future, too, by these three children called mine, and by their practice, the way they move on their mats, so free in their bodies. My littlest girl throws herself into the Three-Legged Dog pose so hard she collapses on her face in a heap of giggles. My son bites his upper lip as he makes a shirtless attempt to nail Lolasana, a nearly impossible pose in which the arms are down and the knees tuck into the chest, levitating as if by some magic and not by the strength of the core. Alan gets the pose. Samara turns cartwheels and works on her handstand holds.

I know, then, that the physicality is the way in. I show them what the body can do, then, just like their mother before them, they will see what the mind can do. They will discover how the spirit can soar and how yoga can pave the way.

I am inspired by the practice and their focus, by the constant hope, fear, pride, and sadness that accompanies almost every day of being a parent. There will be pain and more pain. There will be uncomfortable moments, probably more than a few. There will be graduations, weddings, and births. There will be heartbreak, sickness and tests, and pain and sadness. I know all this. My heart pounds at the thought, and I can't get away from my fears or from my hopes.

This is it. This is the magic. We are only ever promised *this* moment, when we are the oldest we will ever be and the youngest we will ever be. And then it's gone.

Last August, my family did sparklers on the terrace of our lake house in Maine. The older kids are always away at sleepaway camp for the actual Fourth of July, so we celebrate in August. We ate lobsters and blueberry pie. I caught a photo of Alan just as the sunset had started to light up the sky over the lake. The water reflected peach and pink like a mirror, and Alan's eyes are alight with the fire from the sparkler.

Pop! Sizzle! Pop! He holds it away from his body, but his eyes are all in. I know this fire can hurt me, he seems to say. We've all heard the stories: third-degree burns, skin grafts, the horror tales parents pass along, the danger. But, oh, the joy.

His eyes are lit up. His smile is wide and true. I would have missed the moment if I had let the fear win. I would have missed the whole damn thing. It was a mere sixty seconds between the first spark and the last one, the dancing and giggling.

You rarely smell that unique scent of electricity and burning filling up the nostrils, cementing itself somewhere in the brain, filed under "Summer Smells," right beside rainstorms, freshly cut grass, and mildew. Bare feet on the lawn outside camp, fresh worms after a rainstorm, and dirt in the fingernails—it's all part of the experience.

Then the moment ends. The sparkler dies. The sun sets. The last ice cream is licked. The teeth are brushed. The pajamas are put on. The lights go out and there is darkness. The sparkler is a memory from four months ago. It slips through my fingers while my eyes are on something else, something more pressing, something past or future.

This is what we mean by living in the moment. It's all we have.

I see myself at birth, calm, laid on my mother's chest, her breath moving in and out. I hear her heart.

At twelve my head is on her knees. Tears roll down my cheeks. I'm describing a mean friend and a fight. I am scared to go to school the next day, and she doesn't move. "*Shh, shh,*" she says. "Discomfort is the path of growth."

At sixteen I am on a raft. My mother's body is on the dock as I float away, farther from her arms, her chest, and her knees. I take something with me.

At twenty-five I am marrying a man she had predicted I would like all those years before, when I was ten and he was eleven and I hated everything about him.

At twenty-nine I'm a new mom, my own baby on my chest, her rosebud lips so red and perfect.

At thirty-two.

At thirty-five.

And now. This moment. It moves too fast. This is the practice, the way we slow down time. Each breath is a gift, each one an opportunity for reflection, focus, and purpose. What's gone is gone. What's ahead isn't real.

I take each breath as it comes. Here. Now. I am here now.

Guinea Pig Death No. 2

OMG. *Harmony is dead.*

We get a text from our pet sitter while we are sitting at a café in Rome. We have just returned from an all-day bus trip to Pompeii, with a stop at Mount Vesuvius to climb the iconic volcano that buried Pompeii 2,000 years ago. All three kids are hot, tired, and sick of pasta.

I show the text to my husband. We look at Samara, who is twirling a strand of cacio e pepe (cheese and pepper pasta) on her fork, her brow furrowed in concentration. Just minutes before, she'd had a meltdown. "I'm sick of pizza. I'm sick of pasta! I want something different." But nothing else we offer her is better. Beef? No. Salad? No. Mozzarella and tomato? No and no. Pasta it is.

It's three o'clock in the afternoon back home. Lila and Harmony were my daughter's beloved guinea pigs. We bought them for her at the beginning of third grade. We'd created a girl's world just for her in our old master bedroom, with purple walls and white square frames in the center of each one with a deeper purple. We installed a loft bed with a pink desk beneath it and a bookshelf piled high with all the books she's ever read, those she wants to read, and those someone else (me) wants her to read.

She'd told us she was scared to sleep alone, without her brother. Even when they shared a room, she spent most nights in our bed, and we were eager to end that. So Lila and Harmony moved in. Lila, black and white with a patch of brown right up near her ears, was the small one, a bit squat. She looked younger and was much more docile. Harmony was longer, all white, except for a thick belt of black around her middle. She was wild, loving, and rambunctious, running laps across the cage morning, noon, and night.

"They are loud," I told Samara. I could hear them in our new bedroom on a different floor.

"I don't even hear them," she assured me. She did stop coming into our bed, though, which was all we cared about. She'd promised to clean the cage, a monstrosity of wires we had to fill weekly with bits of cardboard bedding, crinkled into tiny balls for their tiny feet to sink into as they walk. The cage had a platform that created two floors, one completely surrounded on three sides to allow for guinea pig privacy.

Their nails grew fast and long, so we were forever clipping them, shivering with fear. It would have been so easy to nick a tiny toe or draw a bit of blood. We held them steady and prayed as we cut. They ate food and pooped at an alarming pace, so we set up standing orders to have little food pellets delivered weekly to our doorstep. They liked treats of carrots, lettuce, and tomatoes.

They needed to be held, so we took them out every day and cuddled them while we watched television. Sam was strict. Her brother and sister were not allowed to take them out without her being present. Not even Rob and I could do so. We were allowed to take them out, but we had to tell her when we wanted to.

"I just want to know where they are," she said.

She needed help cleaning the cages and making sure to feed and water them each morning, but she was fully in charge of these pets. She had asked me to leave the air-conditioning on for them when we left on this two-week trip across Italy.

I told her no, that it was a waste of energy. But now, as I Google, trying to hide my tears from her, I realize that guinea pigs are very heat sensitive and that the heat in her closed room without the air-conditioning probably killed Harmony and might soon kill Lila. There is a heat wave in New Jersey, even for August, and even though we aren't home, I can just imagine the stifling and oppressive air in Sam's bedroom.

I text the sitter:

Turn on the AC right away. Set it to sixty-nine and keep it that way until we get home, even if the heat wave ends. I don't know what we'll tell her. Put the body in the freezer in a Tupperware container.

I look back at Rob. He shakes his head. We wait.

I can't stop crying. We get gelato on the walk home, and the kids don't notice my tears because they are too excited about the options: stracciatella, nocciolo, chocolate. We have tried them all, and on some days we go for it two or three times. Adara's cone is dripping. "Lick! Lick! Lick!" She doesn't, so we pull out the wet wipes and scrub her little hands, but she still creates chocolate handprints on her dress and on each of us.

In the well-lit apartment, Samara notices my face. "What's wrong?"

I tell her, against Rob's wishes, because I know how she'll feel when she does find out. I know what it's like to not be told. She sobs. Alan sobs. I sob. Even Rob cries. Only Adara is confused. "Why everyone crying? Why? Why?"

We promise Sam a new guinea pig. We promise we can have a burial and a ceremony. I am determined to right the wrongs of my childhood, and I think maybe that's why I got her the guinea pigs in the first place. And then Harmony died, so I failed even the simplest of challenges.

Our trip is a few days longer, and we light candles for Harmony in every church we pass. We talk about her and make promises. We will remember the air-conditioning. We will be better and more loving and aware.

Nevertheless, Harmony is dead. The day we return, we open the freezer. Even when you know it's there, a dead guinea pig in the freezer is still a shock. I scream. We put her body on the coffee table. Samara creates a PowerPoint of photos of her, and we sit around and share our favorite memories of Harmony.

"I loved how her nose wrinkled when we gave her carrots."

"I loved how protective she was of Lila. Always going first. Always paving the way."

We drive her to the vet down the street. They will cremate her and return her ashes two days later. Harmony, beloved friend.

Samara smiles and bounces back. She places the ashes on the desk in her room and talks about "Rainbow Bridge," the iconic poem about pet loss that promises that our pets wait for us to die beside the rainbow bridge and that we will be rejoined forever.

"Do you think it's true?" she asks me. "The rainbow bridge?"

"Definitely." That sounds a lot like heaven, and I know I am lying.

I believe in energy, that every living creature has a soul and that Harmony is part of that. But I don't believe we will ever see her again as a whole being, as the black and white sweetheart she was. Her energy has shifted onto another plane. Even though I don't share this with Samara, I think it's just as comforting as the rainbow bridge.

There's a photograph of my mom that came from an old friend. Actually, all I have is a black-and-white contact sheet, one tiny thumbnail photo on a sheet of many. I have to hold it up to the light and run a magnifying glass over to make this one out. My father is in the picture, too, with mutton chops and a paunch. He is much smaller than I have ever known him to be and is sitting on the floor while my mother rests her head in his lap. Friends are laughing, drinking, and smoking.

"That was our apartment on Fifth," my dad says. "Another world. Your mother was twenty-three or twenty-four."

I see her there, her hair long and black. She's smiling, and I know her then. I see the long teeth and the chipped front tooth, so small many might miss it, but I see it every time—a bit of jagged edge where there should be smooth enamel.

She's wearing a peasant top, and her hair is swept to the side. She looks high. Was she high? My father doesn't answer. I've been around enough high people to know. Her eyes are slits but are lit up with possibilities, as if the solution to every problem in the world is just two more tokes away. I use my phone to zoom in close on the small shot of her and create a full photo. She's beautiful, ten years younger than I am now. She's not a mother yet. She doesn't live in Ohio.

"This is when she started taking yoga," my father says.

I can almost smell the cigarette smoke in the room, hanging low, surrounding this group of antiwar activists, smokers, and graduate students. I can hear the conversations and imagine the possibilities, the energy, the pulse of the city and its youth. What a time to be alive.

She falls into yoga by accident, from conversations about energy and our role in the world. There is a fork in the road, and my father takes the path toward material things, like cars and his career. This is a world that can be seen and touched and bought on credit. My mother heads toward mysticism and the spirit and all that happens when you stay open to possibilities and to the wonder of it all.

I wish I could tell them that it will be okay, that they will work despite their different paths and will have a daughter who is equally split between the two, with one foot in *Samadhi* and the other in J. Crew.

But I can tell them nothing because I am not yet born. I am not at that party to watch my mother light up at the many possibilities that will take her far away from her Cleveland home and into something new and fulfilling and more meaningful than anything before it.

"Your mother was a seeker. She just sought the wrong things." This is what her sister Mary tells me. I wonder if she hates my mother for being so wild and so "off." My aunt is a joiner; she was a leftie for years until she moved to the South, where she veered to the right and developed a general disdain for free spirits, which has left her cold and mean and bitter. Her words are impossibly full of every cruel and toxic thing one can say to a young girl who lost her mother so young. I will choose to extricate myself from her, but not without cost. This will create another broken link.

The girl in this picture seems so far away, but we share a face. I post the photo on Facebook.

You are identical, I tell myself. And we are. We have the same high cheekbones, the same full lips, the same rounded chin, and the same thick hair. We share a love of yoga and other, less-than-healthy vices, too.

In twenty years, the girl in this photo will be dead. Would she have lived differently if she had known? Would she have had me sooner? Treated me differently? Become a teacher before her thirties?

In the photo she appears to have all the time in the world. But now she's been dead eighteen years.

Becoming a Woman, Part Two

My period comes in a gush. The anticipation has been years in the making. I am a late bloomer, and I have no idea how to use a tampon or a pad. All my friends, including Janet, start their periods one by one. Some have had it for three years or more. They are growing breasts and catching boy's eyes in bikinis while my chest still looks like a dinner plate.

We've been warned since fifth grade, when they separate boys and girls to tell us what to expect. My teacher says she had a hysterectomy. "Hallelujah!" she exclaims.

Later, when I tell my mother what my teacher said, she is horrified. "She shouldn't have said that. That's gross."

"Why?"

"It just is. We are women. We bleed. It's natural, and she shouldn't make you feel bad about it."

I don't feel bad. I want it to come, but it never does.

"Is this it?" I ask my mother. Day after day I show her my underwear with bits of red string from the seams of the underwear. "Did this come out of me?"

I show her a brown dot that appeared in the crotch. Surely this must be it. I am twelve. I am thirteen. I am fourteen.

"You'll know it when you see it."

Sure enough, the day actually comes. I am two months past my fourteenth birthday, and it comes in a gush of blood. I know it when I see it, just as she told me. I tell my mother and she shimmies her shoulders, getting up to dance around me. "We are going out to celebrate."

She takes me out for dinner, then I watch her give a speech as a board member of Planned Parenthood. We go out for ice cream late, and she reaches for my hand. "You are a woman."

"Finally," I tell her.

"But really. You are now."

I nod. I can't imagine things changing. I am still the same girl I was yesterday. But my mom sees me differently now.

In Portuguese there is a word for the sadness that comes from longing for the past. It's not quite nostalgia. It's more intense than that, more all-consuming. *Saudade*.

My father has spent much of his life doing business in Brazil. He is fluent in Portuguese, and I have recently come back from living there with him over the summer.

"*Saudade*, Mom."

"*Saudade*," she says. "We have to live in the present. No nostalgia. No looking back."

I laugh because my dad is the king of nostalgia. He spends hours listening to old records, reminiscing about old campaign slogans from his glory days in college politics, and hanging out with friends he's known since he was four. *Saudade* is his bag, but my mom knows better.

"We are here. Now."

We are, but I wonder what's so wrong with looking back some-times. The thing about the present is that you never really know how special it is until it's gone. Maybe that's what my mom is getting at. Remember this moment. Mark it. You will never have it again. She takes my hands in hers.

"You are the oldest you have ever been right this second. You are also the youngest you will ever be again. Think about that. This is something you will remember forever. But I hope you feel something different than *saudade*. I hope it shapes you into something other than nostalgic."

"Me too."

The next day I tell my mom I want to try using tampons. She's worried, believing that I should get used to pads and the flow before I graduate to sticking something into my vagina. I insist. All my friends are using them, and I am way behind. I think of the cool girls, sashay-ing about with a long Tampax in their pocket, a source of shame and embarrassment if the wrong person catches it, but something I have envied up until now.

My mother buys me a box of tampons. The most embarrassing part of this, up until today, is that I didn't know there was a hole (my vagina) that is different from my pee hole. I guess I didn't pay enough attention in sex ed, and I haven't been close enough with a boy (unlike my friends, who have), so until this moment in the bathroom, I hadn't actually considered how everything worked down there. Now it seems extra confusing.

I am in my parent's bathroom with a box of pink junior tampons in hand. I figure these will be thin enough to slide into a hole I didn't even know existed up until this moment.

"Take the paper off," my mother says.

That part I understand. I peel the white and pink paper off the cardboard tube, and the thing inside looks like a skinny white cigar with a string hanging from the bottom. I got this.

"Now put the applicator inside and push the bottom up like a Push Pop."

I start giggling. "A Push Pop? Mom!"

But I see her point. It's not a creamy orange treat, but it does have that look. Push Pop it is. I slide the applicator in and only the tip will go in. "Ouch!"

Mom knocks on the door. "What? What hurts? What's 'ouch'?"

"Nothing, I'm fine."

I push it in a little more. "Ouch!"

"Sasha, let's just give you a few cycles before we move on to tampons. Please? Hello?"

I don't answer because I am shoving the tampon in while waving my other hand in the air. Ow. Ow. Ow. Ow.

"It's in!" I pull my pants back up and proudly open the door. But it hurts a lot. This can't be normal.

"Is it supposed to feel so big and poking?"

My mom tilts her head. "No. It's not. What do you feel?"

"A pinch, and it stings a bit."

She starts to troubleshoot. Is it hanging half out? Did I put it in too far? Can I still feel the string?

"No, no, and yes."

She's looking in the trash by the toilet. "Where's the applicator?"

"What applicator?"

"The cardboard tube the tampon came in. Where is it?"

"The paper is in the trash."

Then it dawns on me that the tampon wasn't the whole thing, that the applicator is currently residing inside me. My mother realizes this at the same time. "Pull it out," she orders. Her eyes are a bit wild, which scares me, too. How bad is this? I don't even tell her to leave. I sit on the toilet and begin yanking at the string, but nothing comes out. The pinching gets worse.

"Ow! Ow!" I am crying now. This was a terrible idea. I knew it. I told my mom it was a terrible idea, right? She pushed me into this. I am too young.

She grabs my shoulders and looks me in the eye. "Sasha, I cannot pull this out for you. Relax. Breathe." She is talking to me, but I can see she is talking to herself. She touches her thumbs to her forefingers. A mudra. I do the same. We breathe together. But neither of us is calm. My breath is ragged with panic. I am imagining surgical instruments and doctor's gloves up inside me.

"Get in the bath," she tells me, as she turns the knobs on the Jacuzzi tub. The steam is rising. I take off my clothes and dip a toe in. It's scalding.

"Get in!"

She's yelling, but she softens when she sees my face. "Okay, hold on." She turns the cold water on to run alone and splashes it toward the back. Finally, the water is lukewarm enough for me to get in. "Now just soften your legs. Take Baddha Konasana." I make the soles of my feet touch each other and let my knees butterfly open. The water enters between my legs, and the pinching almost immediately stops.

"Breathe. Breathe. Breathe."

I am breathing. I am using my yoga breath. I am trying.

"Imagine a flower opening. Relax your jaw." She's coaching me. She reaches for my hand. "Blow out your lips like you are a motorboat."

I open one eye and look at her. "Really?"

She nods. "It will help relax you down there."

"Okay." I put my lips together and blow. They sputter. I do it again.

"Now reach for the string."

I hold my breath and pull. It comes out. So does the applicator. My mother is against the stairs leading into the Jacuzzi. She has tears in her eyes and her palms are shaking, but she's laughing.

"It's out! It's out!" I exclaim.

We both cry.

"Well, that was something," she says.

Yes, that was something. "Let's try again?" I ask.

My mom sighs and heads out the door. This time I figure it out. No pain, no sweat. I am a tampon veteran and won't mess up again. My mom comes in and checks the garbage, just to be sure.

I can't know then that fourteen years later, when I go into labor with my first child, when I am deep in the transition between being closed and being open, I will remember this moment. My midwife is sitting beside me. "You are about to meet your baby. You are almost there." My husband is rubbing my back and kissing my neck, whispering words of encouragement. But all I can see is the figure of my mother. I can feel her cool hands on my back, her flat soft palms, the pads of her fingers tickling up my spine. This time she is inside the door, not standing outside. She is reminding me not to bear down, to relax my jaw and allow myself to open, to relax my knees, not to force it out, but to let the baby take her time coming out.

There is no applicator with a baby and no junior size. When all eight pounds of her starts to crown and the burning sensation takes over every part of my body, I see my mother there in front of me, her hands shaking, tears in her eyes. We've been through this before, she and I. We've got this.

The baby slides out, waxy and perfect. She cries right away and opens one eye, staring at me much the same way I am staring at her. The nurses wrap her in blankets and place her on my chest, and she knows what to do. She buries her head there and roots for the nipple, which she finds with her little hungry mouth.

"I'll teach you all of it," I promise. I know this means more than how to drink milk and more than how to insert a tampon, but in this moment, at least, I have everything she needs.

My mother has a granddaughter, although she'll never meet her. My daughter is named for my mother. The moment she is born, I am no longer in the animalistic space between living and dying, and then my mother's presence is gone again. I know that my mother was here the day Samara was born.

"Don't look back and feel sad," my mother told me the day I started menstruating. So I don't. I work to make the past part of the present. *Saudade* 2.0.

Spider in a Jar— Second Time

I have a spider in a jar. As I am cleaning our air conditioner, the spider appears, black and small. It scurries, I scream. I always scream. My toddler looks up from watching a video on YouTube. "What's wrong, Mommy?"

"Nothing, honey. Mommy just saw a spider."

"Ohhh, a spidah?" She pauses the TV and runs over, her bare feet pounding on our wood floor.

"Get me a piece of paper, quick," I tell her, as I question the wisdom of making a curious three-year-old my partner in this. She runs into my study and grabs a piece of lined paper, which she displays proudly in her pudgy hand. She's excited by the drama. "I got it!"

By now I've trapped the spider in a Ball jar. It's crawling up the side, and I take the piece of paper from Adara and lift the jar just enough to slide it under, making sure the spider stays trapped. I fold the paper up and around the jar, holding it tightly closed and walk outside, Adara in tow.

"What now?" she says.

I wonder. Six months ago this would have been impossible. My arachnophobia was so severe I once hyperventilated until I passed out in the basement of my home in Ohio. But now I practice *ahimsa*. Whenever possible I do no harm. I don't eat meat. I don't eat dairy. I don't eat eggs. Now I don't kill spiders.

My old self laughs. My new self makes sure the spider is on the walls of the jar before I take the paper off and tap it until it crawls free. Adara is jumping up and down, clapping her hands.

"We saved her! We saved her!"

I smile. I think we must have, but I also know the reality. Just last week my husband and I came home from a movie through the back door. A spider had spun a web from the ceiling of the first floor all the way down to the base of the deck. It was impressive. My husband and I spent a couple minutes admiring the artistry before we noticed the artist herself sitting at the top of her creation, as big as my hand. Okay, maybe not that big, but close. She was definitely hairy and definitely had spots.

This spider today is small by comparison. It must be a baby, and it has lived inside its whole short life. Can it make it in the backyard with all the giant free-range spiders? Will it be scared, far from its window in our air-controlled home? Out here it's hot, and each blade of grass is a hundred times his size. The world is a cruel place. It's scary and unpredictable.

Did we save the spider? Maybe. We've at least given it a chance. If it dies now, it won't be our fault. "We saved her," I tell Adara, scooping her up in my arms. I hand her the jar and she grins, the gap between her front teeth exposed and perfect. "Mommy, it's time for lunch."

10. Rebirthing

WE ROLL INTO A FETAL POSITION,
REMIND OURSELVES OF OUR INTENTIONS,
EXPRESS GRATITUDE FOR THE PRACTICE AND CHANT.
WE AIM TO REENTER THE WORLD
WITH NEW VISION.

Kripalu Now

God help me. I am in the tempeh line. The other line at Kripalu is for meat eaters. Today the offering is chicken. I am in my fifth month of a vegetarian diet and on my twenty-fifth day of a strict vegan diet. In other words, I have not eaten eggs, any dairy product, or any food with an animal product in it for nearly a month. It's been almost six months since I've had meat. The vegetarian line at Kripalu is always a little longer. People eat mindfully here. And even though there's no shame in eating meat, I feel at home with my fellow plant-based brethren. But tempeh? I wish my mother could see this.

Today's entrée is topped with an apple curry compote, with brussels sprouts and chard on the side and a vegan bread with walnuts and cranberries. Kripalu offers so many condiments, including liquid amino acids, Bragg's nutritional yeast, cardamom, pumpkin seeds, ground flaxseed to garnish everything, and a Kripalu raisin sauce.

The food here is part of the attraction, but nutty tempeh is an acquired taste.

Here I am, eating in the sitting room next to the dining room. I eat all my meals in this beautiful room, where the windows open over the expansive lawn. I watch a single leaf fall from overhead and make pirouettes all the way to the ground. Three geese honk their way through the sky and land to meet their scattered friends at the bottom of the hill, where across the road is a lake. Yesterday I would have seen none of this. I am here on a meditation and writing retreat, but I still struggle with mindfulness. The day before, during our walking meditation, each blade of grass looked amazing. Did grass look like this before, so lush and varied?

I am unconsciously looking for my mother's tree. Is it the tree with the leaves still clinging to it in mid-October? Maybe it's the one with white-tinged bark. I have my doubts whether this one will make it through a New England winter. Only a couple of the trees still have plaques, and I wonder if "in honor of" means the same thing as "in memory of." I doubt it. One is so specific and final. An honor is something else.

My mother's plaque is gone, and I suspect her tree is, too.

I remember a fight from a decade ago. My maternal grandparents visited the tree on their drive back home to Cleveland after visiting us in Boston. The tree was scrawny and diseased. My father, a lawyer, wrote letters in anger. He raged and fumed and yelled and screamed, but I can't remember the outcome. Maybe it's best that I don't, because if her tree is dead and gone, I don't want to know. If it's only the plaque that's missing, then every tree is a possible contender to hold some kernel of my mother.

My father calls me after I leave. "Did you see the tree?"

He always wants to know. Did you hear anything? See anything? Meet anyone? Get any gossip? My dad shares bad news with glee, his mouth practically watering with the prospect of watching an emotional response. He's terminal. *Your aunt died.* He almost seems disappointed when someone else delivers the bad news. I saw him in hospice as my paternal grandfather died, with two phones in his hand. Did you hear? How about you? He makes calls in the middle of the night, even when the news could wait until morning. My great-uncle will still be gone because of a heart attack at the age of eighty-eight even after I have eaten my breakfast and gotten my kids off to school.

I don't think it's a bad thing, at least on my more generous days. I think he wants to be connected and the one watching our responses when the world falls apart. When I was a little girl, he used to sing "The Whiffenpoof Song" to me again and again. *We're poor little lambs who've lost our way.*

I imagined those fluffy, white lambs, endlessly searching for their mamas. *Baa . . . baa . . . baa.* I'd cry and cry.

"It's just a Yale drinking song," he'd say, laughing. Then he'd sing it again.

My father and I have come a long way. His anger and glee aren't malicious, although I used to think so. Why must you scream at airline personnel, insurance agents, and TSA workers? He copes as best he can.

I turn to yoga, meditation, and writing. In my less centered moments I have other coping mechanisms, too, less honorable ones, such as flirtation, margaritas, and the occasional square of white chocolate, laced with a hint of THC. He turns to angry letters and threatening lawsuits.

He spent the last year of my mother's life on the phone. Blue Cross ("the fuckers") denied almost every claim during her second round with cancer. That's how insurance works, or so I was told. Now, at forty, I've just spent a year battling with my insurance company so it would stop denying every claim, so I finally get it. The fuckers.

I used to think I'd never come to Kripalu again because of the sad tree. It hurt my grandparents that the one thing they'd hoped to see for their daughter had withered away to nothing. Now it seems somehow fitting. Whether the tree is here or not, the spirit remains. The smell in the halls is the same. The gift shop is three times the size it was when I started coming here. There are almost a dozen shelves filled with books by authors like Elizabeth Gilbert, Gabby Bernstein, and Oprah Winfrey. The world has taken everything my mother once loved and turned it into a commodity.

Be more mindful. Use your tarot deck to guide your life. Cook vegetarian food. The Kripalu gift shop does not sell Lululemon's products, but I see them on a lot of women in my workshop and even on some of the teachers in the 300-hour programs. Consumerism has come to Kripalu, and suddenly this place is trendy.

"I am dying to get there," a friend says on Facebook. "Everyone I know says they love it."

It's "in" now—the vegan food, the Ujjayi breath, the meditation. Mindfulness is so now. Instagram has changed yoga, too. Now impossibly thin women with rock-hard abs create ten-second videos in which they leap into handstands and wave their legs like it's nothing. Yoga teachers have become celebrities, with millions of followers hanging on their every word. There are hundreds of yoga clothing companies that sell $100 leggings covered in everything from hamburger prints to Christmas trees. I currently have eighty-one pairs of yoga leggings. I am not proud.

The guru is gone. The spirit remains.

Kripalu yoga is still a slow and mindful practice. The hot studios in my New Jersey town call themselves yoga, but they aren't in the same league at all. People leave during Savasana.

"I have to get to preschool pickup," they say, as they roll up their mats and jump into their Range Rovers in their $300 yoga outfits. At Kripalu, Savasana is never under five minutes. It is silent. There is no pop music. Often there is no music at all. Just your hands on the mat, your breath, and the breathing of your neighbor. You go to that place.

I take the tempeh and smile. Never say never, I think. My tray is piled high with veggie goodness. I sit in the dining room and chew a thousand times. Each bite is for my mother. If she could see Kripalu now, would she love it as much? She would. Maybe even more.

Reiki, Level One

"If you are a seer, you will see again," Carol tells me.

We are in a Reiki attunement class as part of my ongoing training as a yoga teacher. My boss and friend at the main studio where I work is a level-three Reiki healer, and she has brought in her teacher, Carol Anne, to lead the rest of us through this training.

Reiki is a form of alternative medicine that involves a master who has gone through three levels of attunement, learning to use his or her energy to move the energy in another person's body. For a yoga teacher, Reiki is a piece of the wellness puzzle. It is a way of moving the energy that centers around our chakras, the seven wheels of energy that run up the midline of the body and control so much of our past and present. When we practice yoga, whether we know it or not, we move the energy in a similar fashion. But certain poses are better at balancing certain chakras, and a teacher who works in all these modalities has so much more power and ability to help and heal.

It's an important part of my training. Carol is explaining that each of us will experience the energy field in different ways, depending on our individual gifts. Some may hear spirit voices, "guides" who help identify where the energy needs to move. Others will feel it in their hands as a vibration that shows where the energy needs to shift and change. Others will see it.

"Look back into your childhood and remember," Carol instructs.

One woman recalls that she could hear spirits as a child, but her mother asked her to stop, so she lost the ability. I remember that day with Mrs. Vaughn, seeing the blue and the red and knowing to my core that what I was seeing was more than just in my head.

"I used to be able to see auras," I volunteer.

Carol Anne nods at me. "Then you will see them again," she promises.

And I believe now that I will. I believe it because my mom believed in me then. Sometimes that's all it takes.

Men Who Hate Yoga

My husband doesn't enjoy yoga. It pains me to type these words, because otherwise we are an annoyingly happy couple who shares everything. But he hates the heat, the spirituality, and the focus on slow movement and breath. He even hates Savasana.

Hating Savasana really should have been a deal breaker. After all, corpse pose is the reward for an hour or more of hard work. To collapse in a pool of your own sweat and let your bones settle themselves into the ground while you listen to light chimes, an Andean flute, or sometimes just blessed silence is the most delicious part of any good class. But he hates it.

"I like the stretching, and I will come for that. But it's not a workout," he says.

I disagree. Yoga tones, flattens, strengthens, and lengthens every part of the body. But it's more than that, too. A regular practice strengthens and tones the mind and the spirit. When I say this, he laughs, and I cringe.

Rob attends my classes once a month, miserable and sweating, allowing me to adjust his body and move his thigh so it's closer to the "parallel to the earth" position we like to get into in Warrior Two. My husband is strong, an avid athlete who was a Division One decathlete. He likes to move his body and be active, so yoga might not be his bag, and he claims to hate it, but he's also not against it.

My father, in contrast, moves only when he is in a city and has to walk from place to place. Otherwise he prefers to be on the couch, book in hand. He would never try yoga. It wasn't just Gurudev's parking spot, either. It was the breathing, the chanting, and the strange movements. He would mock my mother in the kitchen and make jokes about the practice. It was funny to him. I joined in on the fun because that's what our family did. We mocked. We took aim at my father's weight, too, his love of all things fried and fatty, and his weird obsession with his high school friends and love of musicals.

Everything was fair game in our house. Every compliment came with a teardown.

"You are pretty, except for your thick neck," my father told me when I was sixteen. By then my skin was as thick as my neck allegedly was, and I was only semibothered. More than a decade of dinner-table ribbing had prepared me to take a hit without tears.

All of this is the opposite of yoga. Whereas yoga is soft and kind, my family was hard and harsh. We always pushed buttons and mocked.

"I have a great idea," my father would say at the dinner table. "Let's go to bed early tonight." My father is always tired. Later we learned he has a severe case of sleep apnea, but then it was a family joke that his snoring vibrated throughout the house, which it did. My room is separated from his by a long hallway, three bedrooms, and a bathroom, yet I could still hear his snores, sometimes at midnight.

"You always want to go to bed early," I tell him, rolling my eyes. My mother looks at me, smiling. "I have an idea. Let's stay up until nine o'clock," she says in a voice four octaves deeper than her own, mocking his tone. I throw my head down on the table and pretend to snore, growling from so deep in my throat that I choke and laugh at the same time. We all are laughing by now, even Dad, who raises his eyebrows.

"What? What? Who wouldn't want to go to bed early?"

My parents were opposites and have always known this. They each have a study in our house. My mother's, where she practiced, is light and airy. The carpet is white and the walls are light blue. Every book on the shelf is either spiritual or feminist and sometimes both. If you want a copy of *Writing Down the Bones* or *A Course in Miracles*, check out my mother's study.

My father's study faces the back of the house, where the light almost never seems to shine. There is a TV in his study, but it sits on wheels and you have to get up to change the channel. The walls are a deep dark red, and the carpet is dark brown. Every wall is covered in bookshelves. The books are lined up, one after the other, and when there is no more room on a shelf, he piles other books on top, in the space between the tops of the books and the next shelf up. The effect is dizzying, from floor to ceiling—books on top of books on top of books. A friend and I once tried to count them. We lost track at a thousand. This is before the show *Hoarders*, but when it first aired, I thought of my father and his books. A bibliophile or a hoarder? Sometimes it's hard to tell.

Not a single one of his books is spiritual. There is Brazilian history and an older copy of *Mein Kampf*. There are countless books on World War II, the Holocaust, and the Jewish people. There are at least twenty copies of a book our Israeli cousin wrote in the early 1980s that my dad bought in bulk to give away to his friends. In one corner of the room sits his large desk, a gift from his father after he graduated from law school. It's perpetually covered in stacks of papers.

"How do you know where anything is?" my mother says.

"I just do."

My mother was Marie Kondo, the famous organizing expert, before Marie Kondo. The joke in our house is that no piece of mail, no matter how precious, is safe on any counter. Once it has sat idle for more than a day, it is subject to my mother's fits of trash-happy behavior. She goes through the house like an anteater, only instead of snorting ants into her nose she sweeps errant items into a giant garbage bag. Leftover food, toys, papers, single shoes—nothing is safe when she is in one of her moods. More than once I have found only a single shoe after one of her sprees because the other went out with the trash the week before.

The biggest fight I ever saw my parents have was over this difference between them. My father was helping me once with a school project and went into the garage to find a box of campaign buttons and posters from elections in the 1960s. Some of the posters were personal, from his campaign for student body president at Bowling Green State University in 1967, and some of them were from national and local elections. The box wasn't in the garage or in the basement, either.

"Have you seen that box of old campaign posters?" my father asked my mother, after looking for at least an hour.

"What did it look like?"

I was standing behind my dad and could see her face. She knew where they were, and the answer was not going to be good.

"Like a box," my dad said. "I don't know. It may have been brown."

"Was it kind of falling apart and water-damaged in the corners?" She sounded hopeful, as though she could spin this as their being ruined anyway.

"Maybe." He looked at her. "You fucking threw them out, didn't you?"

She wasn't sorry. She shrugged. "They were old and dusty. If you wanted them, you should have kept them somewhere else."

My father didn't yell. He's not a yeller. But he does mope—a lot: hanging his head down, shuffling his feet, and mumbling about those campaign buttons and what they might be worth to collectors and on eBay. Even now he occasionally laments the loss.

"That one time your mother pitched all my legacy. If only I had those posters." He will repeat this wistfully, again and again, throughout my childhood, and I will wonder what it would be like if he had them. Then what? This is worse than yelling. Later I struggle at the apex of their competing philosophies. I am a hoarder and a purger at the same time, a person who saves every letter and note anyone ever wrote to me from the age of five but who also throws out clothing before I have even worn it.

Of course this isn't the only way my parents are different. This juxtaposition can be seen in their bodies as well. My father is corpulent. He has a round belly that protrudes far over his pants and requires extra belt holes to contain. My mother's frame is bony, her wrists so small that even my twelve-year-old thumb and forefinger can make a circle around each one and still touch. She has a graceful clavicle. My mother and I look alike. People tell me this all the time, and it annoys me. I want my own face—my own nose and my own cheekbones. Instead I have hers.

"You look like your mother made a Xerox copy." Years from now my father will point out that it's not really an exact match when he references my fat neck, but he's wrong. It's exact, and eerily so. When I look at my hands, I see hers, graceful, with long fingers and pop-out veins. I keep my nails longer than hers and always painted, but when they are bare and short they round out in dramatic ovals, just like hers. Her cheekbones are high, almost Native American, and mine are, too. We have the same smile, the same thick hair, the same laugh, and the same easy way with our bodies. When my grandfather, her father, was dying in 2004, he called me by her name and took comfort in telling me stories of "my" childhood in Cleveland, with him as my father.

"Don't tell him the truth," my grandmother whispered, gripping my hand as tears streamed down our faces.

There are differences, too. I am five foot five, depending on how straight I am standing. My mother is somewhat tall at five foot eight. I am curvy and rounder than she ever was, and my breasts are two sizes bigger. She is bony, angular, and small. "The skinniest mom in our school," my friend Nikki calls her. But that doesn't make it less embarrassing when she wears a yellow Dick Tracy trench coat and refuses to shave her legs.

It never even occurs to us that my father might try a different path, that he might choose to try one yoga class or maybe even two. There is a reason it matters to my mother. It never occurs to any of us that when she is throwing things away, she is trying to practice nonattachment. All the things in our home—the Gorman paintings, the books, the Jacuzzi tub—are just "stuff." What really matters is the way we talk to one another and the way we interact.

"Did you ever try yoga?" I asked my father last week, twenty-five years after her death.

"No," he says, looking at me as though he's wondering what I am thinking. Maybe there is a bit of guilt here, too—the things he should have done, could have done, would have done, if he had it to do over again. But then he shakes it off. "She tried to teach me to meditate once. But I couldn't sit cross-legged."

And so my father and my husband, two men with entirely different worldviews, religious beliefs, careers, and mentalities, can bond over this one thing. They both hate yoga. But I will never stop trying to lead them down the path.

Practicing with Samara

Samara is ten, finally old enough to practice with me. She and I wear matching leggings when we do. We have two pairs: pink and black, and blue and black. Today, we have the blue and black pairs on. She's wearing a long black top, and I am in a black tank top.

It's the summer solstice celebration by the pool deck at the studio where I teach. Samara is excited. We choose a spot just beside the pool. The sun is setting in a bright blue sky with only a few wispy clouds in whimsical shapes. We watch before class starts.

"Look, mommy a polar bear! A kite! A monkey!"

I see them all and point to some of my own: a small dragon, an open book, and a diamond ring.

Samara reaches for my hand as we start the meditation. We are seated inches from the pool. The water sloshes into the filter. A soft audible breeze accompanies Samara breathing beside me. In, out. Inhale, exhale.

In two days she will leave for sleepaway camp. I feel my chest tighten at the thought. It's her third summer at Chimney Corners, a

camp in the Berkshires in western Massachusetts, just twenty minutes away from Kripalu. The camp is magical: a beautiful month of
silly girls, running, jumping, laughing, and playing. They learn to
kayak and swim long distances. They make T-shirts and pottery, put
on musicals, and learn how to release an arrow so strong that it flies
in a perfect arc right into the bull's-eye.

It's her favorite place, and I know she's thinking of it now as she
holds my hand in meditation. I know she wants to get on with it.
Tomorrow is the last day of school, and then we will start to pack,
hauling two large trunks out of the attic—one for her and one for
Alan, who goes to Camp Becket, just down the road. Packing will be
insane, as it always is: shouting, forgetting things, realizing we need to
run to the store for the eighteenth time in one day. Then they will be
gone. The house will be silent, except for Adara, who will ask "Sissy?
Bro-bro?" every five minutes and nearly break my heart.

I know this is ahead, so I squeeze Samara's hand, which roots me
in the present. Her hand is warm and vaguely sticky against my own,
and nearly the same size. She has surpassed me already in her feet
by one size. I know height is on the horizon. She's long and lean, and
her father is tall. It's only a matter of time. The changes are happening slowly. She stays in her room more now and joins the family less.
She's quieter. There are fights with friends, and she snaps at her little
sister more than before.

I look at her perfect face: no lines, no wrinkles, no blemishes
of any kind—a clean slate. The breeze is blowing her hair, and if I
squint I can almost see the child she was and the woman she will
become—both at the same time in this one perfect moment. That's
where we are right now.

The meditation ends, and we start to move. I am focused, except when I'm not. I watch Samara in my periphery, gliding through Surya Namaskara A (Sun Salutations Group A). Her body moves so easily into the posture. I don't need to adjust her or explain anything. She just knows. It's instinctive for her, like water moving through a channel. This hand here, this foot there.

I remember her in her first yoga class when she was four. The small studio was down the street from our condo in Boston, with gorgeous light and three pillars in the middle of the space. I wondered how people could practice there, where you can see everything on the street: people hurrying to pick up their dry cleaning, picking up Peruvian chicken, or getting their oil changed. As I tell my students, forget the noise outside. Listen to the noise in your head. Maybe the distraction is part of the magic, giving an extra boost to mindfulness. Pay no attention to the bustle outside the window. We are here, now.

In what seems like a lifetime ago, during every school vacation, I packed Samara and Alan into a trailer on the back of my bike and pedaled them across town for a yoga camp. Samara's hair was curly and hung down to her waist. Alan, so blond, reached his tiny hands up for me. "Mommy, I wuv! Mommy, I wuv!" He's the most affectionate of my children, the most in love with his mommy. He's so easy compared to Samara. She loves me, too, of course, but cautiously, from a more guarded place.

"Mommy," she typically says, her eyes narrowed, her head tilted, always questioning, wondering why I do the things I do, as though she's watching me for clues about who she'll be one day. I know she is doing this, because I did it, too. Watching my mother's hands as she cooked, I wondered if I would chop like that. Will I knead dough that way, slapping it down, punching it, and turning it over?

My children were so little then that they shared one yoga mat. The yoga camp was perfect, with half an hour of yoga and then song, dance, games, and snacks. "I love yoga," Samara declared, twirling through the living room, her waist-length hair trailing her like a tail.

She still loves yoga, but it's different now. She knows all the poses. She can stay focused for a full hour. Her thigh is perfectly parallel to the Earth in Warrior Two. She can sit in the lotus position for hours, placing her hands outside her hips and picking up her knees, again and again.

"See, Mommy? See?" she says in that way daughters do. I know it because I did it, too. *Look at this young body. Look how easy it is to do things you can't do.* But it doesn't make me sad. It doesn't make me feel inadequate. Tears prick my eyes. I wish my mother could see. I wish she could see what her granddaughter can do.

My children love the challenging poses. Alan wants to be able to do all the arm balances and inversions. Samara throws herself into handstands and forearm stands and giggles when she falls. I envy that confidence so much. I still can't practice a handstand away from a wall because my fear of falling is so great.

Start them while they are young, I was told, when they still have no fear. This is what I see in my children: no fear, no self-consciousness. But I know it's coming. I try to fight it with yoga and mindfulness.

The study Rob and I share is cluttered with papers, books, toys, and old Halloween decorations. We've long since given up the dream of sitting at the desks in there and working, because it's become a catch-all for all kinds of miscellaneous items that don't have a home anywhere else in the house.

There is also an almost embarrassingly large collection of yoga gear: seven heavy cork blocks I bought when I thought I'd be teaching more private classes; two purple foam blocks, soft enough to use as pillows during practice; ten yoga mats. The pink Baptiste mat is thin and worn, the "Sasha" I scrawled in Sharpie at O2 Yoga barely perceptible after so many years of sweat and tears, hot air, and essential oils. There is my blue Manduka mat, thick and heavy, at least eight pounds of marbled blue polyvinyl chloride (PVC). This is the mat I use at home. It never pulls or turns up in the corners. It never trips me. It's soft and cushioned for knee-down poses, like Anjaneyasana (low lunge).

The black Manduka Pro mat is usually at the front because I use it daily, carting it back and forth to class in a handmade black yoga bag with embroidered chakra symbols in bright rainbow colors. This mat smells of rubber, sweat, and mildew. Three years of daily use will do that. The tight roll and mat bag still look brand-new. Every other morning, on sunny days, I take it to the back deck and spray it down with Thieves essential oil, hoping it will remove the smell. It never does. But to part with this mat would be too hard. I keep it and use it despite the smell.

There are five other mats. Samara won one as part of a raffle at one of my studios. There's the mat I bought when I forgot mine and couldn't bear to practice on one of the studio mats. And there's the mat I travel with whenever I go out of town; it's green and folds up like paper in the bottom of a suitcase.

The study is full of other accessories: an impractical wool yoga blanket that cost more than $100 and now sits under my desk, collecting cat hair; a purple bolster that props feet and knees and provides support in the Hero pose (sitting with the buttocks between the heels and leaning backward). There are two straps, countless bags and totes, and at least a hundred yoga books, such as *Strala Yoga*, *Aim True*, *Yoga Anatomy*, *Hot Yoga*, the Bhagavad Gita, and *The World Peace Diet*.

My favorite accessory is one of the least useful: the green mat, which is at least six years old. It's made of cheap foam and almost never lies flat. It's shorter than all my mats by at least a foot, and there is a scene painted on it of children under a tree, dancing and playing musical instruments, with one child standing beside the tree. This was Samara's first mat. At this point it's Adara's. She's nearly four. If you ask her what her favorite activity at preschool is, she always answers the same way: "It's yoga! I love to do yoga!"

She does. She does Downward Dog in the kitchen while we make dinner. She walks her little feet up the archway that separates the dining room from the living room and holds an L-shaped handstand. She lifts one leg into a perfect Three-Legged Dog and opens her chest into a perfect Cobra. The yoga they learn in school isn't vinyasa. The poses all have animal names. She says her favorite is Giraffe. But she also loves Tiger, Flamingo, and Snake. I can imagine these poses in my mind, but when she shows them to me, slithering across the floor, I get the appeal of being belly down and moving in whatever way feels good.

It's not about perfect posture or understanding vinyasa for these kids. It's about presence and creativity of movement—a love of one's body and all that it can do.

During the practice by the pool, Samara looks over at me and smiles. "Still here?" she mouths.

As if I could be anywhere else. But I think she means I am staring. I am not practicing. I am watching her, gliding, moving, and breathing, each pose so natural in her ten-year-old body. I nod. "Still here," I whisper. And I am. Always.

The best mornings are the ones when the mist comes off the lake and fills the entire space between Kripalu's enormous main building and the lake at the bottom of the hill. The mist fills in the forested areas between the lake and the road and then crawls across the lawn, teeming with life. It comes all the way up to the terrace, accessible from the Kripalu lobby.

On this morning I am taking a run at 5:05 AM. My sister and my aunt Patti are back in the room, sleeping. I am the only one up on our floor. The pink bathroom is empty, which gives me time to be alone. This is key when you are sharing a bathroom with a hundred other people. I take my time. I run my hands across the tiles and splash cool water on my face.

As I go down the stairs, I notice the silence ringing in my ears. At Kripalu breakfast is a silent meal, but there is always sound: the shuffle of feet across the floor, the clop-clop of a fast walker, the jingle of spoons against knives and forks, the clatter of trays being set down, the whir of a conveyor belt taking dirty dishes to the kitchen, the clink of a spoon stirring hot tea, and the scraping of chairs being pushed away from tables.

I love this. I have my iPhone and my earbuds. My sneakers are untied, but I'll fix that when I get to the terrace. I am ready to run, ready to listen to loud music and pound the pavement, my heart beating in my ears.

My Aunt Patti, my sister Mariel, and I are on one of our annual trips to Kripalu. It's our weekend to get away and be together. We manage it for a few years before life gets in the way and we all become too busy or too globally scattered. This annual weekend serves another purpose, too. It's unstated, unplanned, and obvious. We remember.

I walk out the back door. There is silence: no cars, no people, no slosh of coffee in a cup. Nothing. I've never been able to stand silence. It feels like secrets, like truths unspoken, like a waste of time. If there is no sound, there is no discussion, no greater purpose, no exchange of ideas, no learning.

"You talk too much, you never shut up," my friend Stacey used to sing in middle school and high school. She and a few other friends called me "the Chat." There was always something to say or discuss, something to ponder. I like to hash it out, prattle, and yack. I walk into the mist, and within a few steps the door back to Kripalu isn't visible. This is a special kind of New England mist, and I feel grateful to witness it. It's thick. It's ubiquitous. It's crawling up the stairs and filling my lungs. This is some Stephen King–level thing here. No one writes better about New England.

I am not scared of clowns, murderous toddlers, or killer laundry machines. I am not scared of old graveyards, history, or tombstones that predate the American Revolution. I am not scared of the mist. There are much scarier things that can happen, and I know this intrinsically. They happen naturally over time. It's not the killer beneath the bed that gets you, statistically speaking.

I choose not to run or turn on my music today. This is so unlike me. There is no sound, not even my footsteps. I glide across the grass silently, seeing only a few feet in front of me, placing one foot in front of the other.

I am underneath a low-hanging cloud. I fight the urge to check the weather. Will this lift? Will we be able to take the long bike ride we planned later in the day? In New England they say, "If you don't like the weather, wait a few minutes." It took me a long time to figure out that people say that everywhere. This is a yogic moment, I think. I tell my students not to ask how many breaths are left but to take each breath as it comes. One foot in front of the other. One breath rolling in, just in time to roll back out.

This cloud is serious, though. Walking isn't so much a choice as it is a necessity. If I tried to run I might hit a tree or a car or trip over a rock. This mist is rooting me in the moment, and I can't fight it.

I walk down to a path to the lake. The mist is already rising. I can see ten feet ahead of me, then twenty, now even more. I slide my phone into my back pocket and walk, as though I am being pulled. At the lake I resist the urge to slide my phone out of my pocket and photograph this moment. This desire is laughable, really. I am alone here. With no kids, no friends, no distractions. Yet instead of being in this moment, I want to post it to Instagram. Look at me! I can't stand to be alone, even for a few seconds. It's not about the bragging or the showing off. It's something else.

If I sit here long enough, I start to remember. I am sixteen. I am in my bathing suit. My mother is on her back, her hair short and gray. The soles of her feet are rooted in the sand, her white knees pointed up to the sky. Mariel is splashing in the water, and the air is getting cooler, even in August.

"Come back in," I call to Mariel. "It's getting cold."

I can see even from here that her lips are blue and she's shivering and yet my mom is lying on her back. Why doesn't she care? Why doesn't she get up?

I am angry about the past and in the present. That sense of loneliness reaches across time. It catches me even in moments when I am not alone. When I was still on speaking terms with my Mary, mother's other sister, she made me a promise. "When you get married and have children, the pain will lessen and you will feel less lonely."

I carried this promise with me, like something I could count on. It will get better. It became a mantra. And yet here we are. I have a

husband and three kids, but it's not better. And now I know. She was
wrong about this, too.

Sometimes I feel ashamed of this grief, as though there is something wrong with me for endlessly missing her. We all lose our mothers. This is the natural order. And yet it isn't. It's not natural to lose her
at sixteen. It's not natural to lose her at seven (my sister's age when
she died).

This loneliness is the price. It's like a rounded chunk of ice cream
scooped right from my center. I'll never be normal. I'll never be
whole. It never really goes away. And yet I am happy. I am in love. I
have so much to be grateful for. These truths coexist.

Yoga means "to yoke," to connect, to bring together the divine
and the profane. People interpret it in their own way. Some think it
means community, connecting with those around us in meaningful
and soulful ways. Others think it means the union of the body and
the soul. I think it means all those things and then some.

The loneliness and the connection, the love and the pain, are all
connected, and each one enhances and enriches the other. A friend
told me recently that discomfort is the human condition and we need
to embrace it.

We use our cell phones to escape. I post to Facebook when I am
feeling down, when the quiet is too much. See, I am interesting. I have
things to say. It's the hand across the darkness, the connection we all
crave. But it lacks soul.

I know why I need my practice. The loneliness is there. But so is
the magic.

Acknowledgments

Red Smith, the sports writer at *The New York Times* is often credited with this famous quote about writing: "Writing is easy. You just open a vein and bleed." And though there is some controversy over whether he is the originator of those words, the truth is that any writer could have said the same. Writing this book was difficult at times, brutal at others. I miss my mother every day, but my relationship with her is complicated by distance and time and the eyes of an adult that now see what my child eyes never could. She was complicated. I am complicated.

To Mariel, my sister and biggest cheerleader: You are the greatest gift from mom. I am so grateful to have you in my corner and adore you more than you will ever know.

To my three children, Samara, Alan, and Adara: You are my life, my love, my reminder not to take things so seriously. Your unconditional love is the only kind I need and I hope someday you will read this book and know that a mother's love transcends time, distance, and even death.

To my best friend, Mackenzie who let me sleep in her guest bedroom, tear my hair out, cry over e-mail and text, and who still read through my pages with love and support: I am so very thankful every day that my silver Doc Martens brought us together more than twenty years ago.

To my father: Thank you for letting me do the hard work of telling my own story with (minimal) complaining. Memory is fluid and subjective and I love you.

Thank you Edy for being the grandmother my children adore and for giving me the space to tell my story.

To my Aunt Patti: Thank you for all the letters and memories of my mother that helped me remember all the things it would have been easy to forget.

To all the writers (you know who you are) who assured me that vomiting after writing was normal and feeling like it would never be done was not a sign it never would. I am so grateful to have so many successful and smart women in my corner who know exactly how much goes into a memoir and how very much it is like bleeding onto the page.

Thank you to Roberta Zeff, my editor at the *New York Times*, who bought the essay that became this book and helped me edit it into something I was so proud to see in print that eventually led me to Allison Janse, my amazing HCI editor who made this dream into a reality.

To my editor, David Tabasky, I am humbled by your creativity and your ability to see the forest through the trees. Thank you for "getting" my work and believing in it without fail.

I could not have written this book without the unwavering support of my husband who sent me away for weekends at a time again and again so I could write in peace. I am a high maintenance writer who needs total silence and a room of my own to get words on the page and I am endlessly grateful to have a partner who gets that. I believe that my mother had a hand in bringing us together and I am grateful to every lucky star in the universe that we found our way into each other's hearts. Thank you. Thank you. Thank you.

About the Author

Sasha Brown-Worsham has been writing since birth and has served as lifestyle editor both at Café Mom and She Knows, Inc. Her essays have appeared in the *New York Times, Cosmopolitan, Boston Globe, Self, Parents*, and many other publications over the years. She lives with her husband and three children outside of London, England. *Namaste the Hard Way* is her first book.